THE
KINDEST LIES

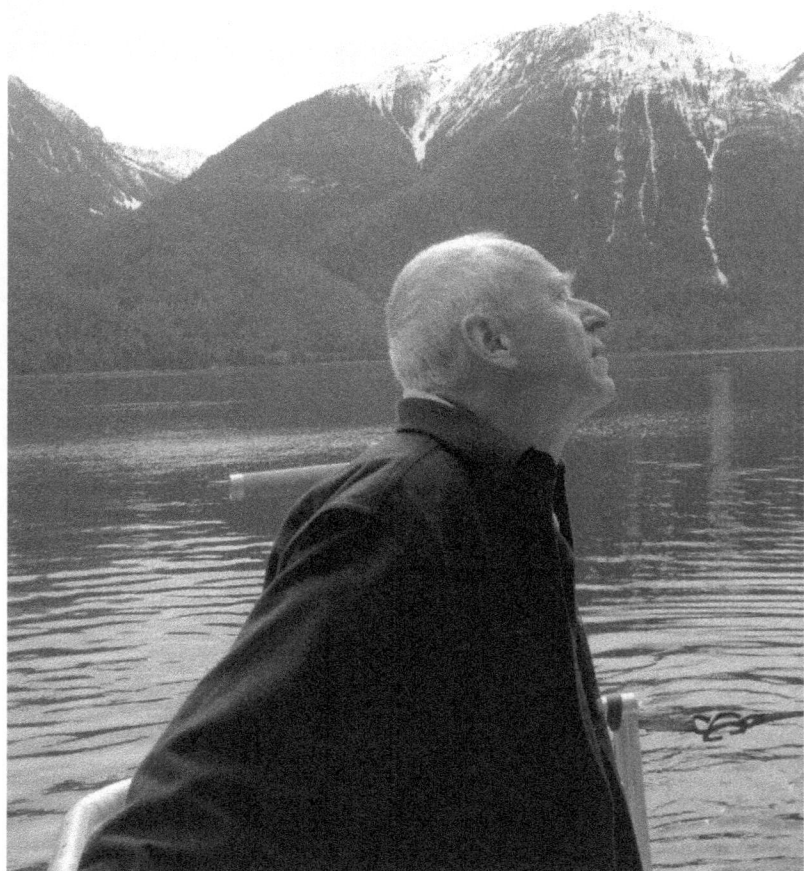

THE
KINDEST LIES
THE LYRICS OF JOHN LYLE

JOHN LYLE

LEAKY BOOT PRESS

The Kindest Lies: the Lyrics of John Lyle
by John Lyle

First published in 2013 by
Leaky Boot Press
http://www.leakyboot.com

ISBN: 978-1-909849-01-3

THE RECORDINGS OF JOHN LYLE

He Knows Who He Is by Matt Bialer	7
Golden Blast of Never	11
Wild Awake	15
Known Corners	31
Cool Fire	43
Down the Road and Far Away	55
Too Late To Panic	67
Almost Like Fate	77
Beauty Looks Away	89
Humors	95
Hard Cover Virgins	105
Bootleg Powerhead	125
Singles	139
The Kindest Lies by Cynthia Atkins	161
Index of First Lines	164
Index of Song Titles	168

♪ HE KNOWS WHO HE IS

A foreword by Matt Bialer

John Lyle is like a ghost drifting in the wind. That's what I think his lyrics say to me. Of course, all great lyrics and works of art say many different things to different people. John's lyrics say a lot to me in low whispers.

I could imagine a young, impressionable John hitching rides on freight trains, wide eyed at the diversity of the land and its peoples. Perhaps he would have written a lyric very much like This Land is Your Land/This Land is My land and we would all be happier for it.

Like a ghost drifting in the wind.

The John Lyle of these lyrics is no less spiritual about the land. But he's a man often alone in a desert. Just as the wind lashes against the ancient rocks and underbrush and carves raw beauty, John's heart has been ravaged by love and loneliness. His raspy, reedy voice rises, sings and celebrates the unspeakable and the unknowable. For all of the beauty of these songs, they are also elegies.

John Lyle is a troubadour in the purest sense of the word: One of a class of lyric poets and poet-musicians, often of knightly rank. John Lyle is indeed a knight.

For 39 years, he was actually a postman. I asked him if he had the same route for the whole time. I could easily imagine that. He said that he did not. But he liked to keep the same route for as long as he could.

The Poet Postman quietly observing people as he delivers their bills, their hardship, dreams and revelations. He never fails to show up, at least in my mind. Woody Guthrie could appreciate that. And so could Mr. Cohen and Mr. Dylan. Being a postman is the perfect source for lyrics.

I know who I am
I know why I'm here

It's like baking bread every morning. John's songs are the bread of the earth. They are the simple, spare nourishment that we all need to survive.

When one reads the lyrics and listens to the music of John Lyle there is no doubt that one feels this is a man, an artist and human being that knows who he is.

He doesn't like to perform live. That is not who he is.

Like a ghost drifting in the wind.

In 1972, he sat next to Joni Mitchell on a ferry. There were only two other people on the boat: the boat operator and Jackson Browne. Joni and and Browne were fighting so she came over and sat next to John. Neither one of them spoke to each other. John was not going to speak.

I know who I am
I know why I'm here

The singer Paul Rodgers of Bad Company fame was on his route. John left a cd of his songs in his mailbox and then didn't say a word. One day Rodgers saw John and told him how much he enjoyed his songs. Nothing more ever came of it.

John is a wistful ghost. But he always takes a breath, a breath of light.

As a ghost, he likes the shadows, that misbegotten shadow.

Not but a shadow
Held my world of stormy care

There is never time to waste in this holy place, which is this land we live in. This life, this vast landscape of the heart. Those are John's words and Woody would concur and so would all of the great poets.

The valley might be lonesome and the blossoms might be broken but to John Lyle they will always scent the morning air. Always. And to me, this lies at the heart of John's art.

The mourning dove might be mourning but he is also rising with that boundless love. All that is closed is open wide.

He is the Sage Postman.

What I love about the poetry of John Lyle is that in any desert there is always a river to be found — even if it is deep underground. He knows what the source of high art is.

You can take my heart
But the loving part will not disappear

John Lyle is like a ghost drifting in the wind.

Matt Bialer
Brooklyn, New York
May, 2013

GOLDEN BLAST OF NEVER

An Introduction

Something gets fixed in your eye that you want to do and it turns around and blinds you So you turn back like a clock and try something totally unnatural and alienating to reverse the flow to somewhere like it was when it started out. That doesn't really work but you do it anyway just to do something because it's impossible to do nothing in this world. You want to get rid of all the reams of bug-eyed hangers on who would do anything for you but can't even tie their shoelaces in your presence. And you know that all-consuming love is so close to rage that it's got them backed up against a wall so hard and so deep it burns to the heart of who they think they are. And any second now they could turn into your biggest fan and blow out the great white light they think annihilates their own sense of being. But everything you do is right for them and wrong for you and it drives you forty bad miles down a dead end road where the masked bandits of the cross lay in wait for the dead pan desperation slashed across your brow. And you make that deal at that twisted crossroads of the mind and buy all they have of that dead certainty only the truly insane lay out as the word and the way. And those who loved you can't anymore because the power that is no power at all has turned you into a monster of desire so fragile in your motion that everyone and every-thing must come to you without seeing you, and bow to your steel clad heels til the brutal wind of tomorrow blows them like chaff to the dirty shoulders of your life.

I have sacrificed my nerves in the crucible of their shrill tones, splitting the cavernous nights right down the middle of

11

what I thought I was doing. I only wanted to be johnny b goode, and then it all caught fire and I felt small but I wanted to make myself big. I tried to compete but could only steal, until that bug under my lunging tongue bit so hard I understood I was not there to understand. From then on, one message to deliver; but no way to keep on after the first chance was taken away as all chances are. I took up the ukelele and built my house of stone. A squirrel passed through the gates and shattered my endless heart, but only for the moment.

I struck at the fools with the only weapons I had; my ancestry cool and forebearing with the survival instincts of the cockroach and the bear, driven to landfills where ragged souls live and play the music of Fats Domino who made it big, big big, and my childish wit, dancing on the stars with the righteous knowledge that I and I alone had found what needed to be said. With at least a ghosted chance and the resignation of the damned, I broke down and did a small tour where I fooled myself into thinking we choose what we believe. I had the posture of a snail and the lion-hearted dream of the ghetto being something more in my own time. But I wrapped myself in my own flag and that of my people while burning all the rest, not knowing it cannot be had all ways. I was stuck in the dual nature of a joke that cannot be told by itself. I laughed only when they laughed. I didn't mean to hurt anybody, but I did and said I was joking and any fool could see that, if he'd only open his eyes and understand I was turning it all upside down so the lies would fall out. But it didn't work because it never could work that way. I spiraled into a vortex of bitter dreams that broke my pen and left me with only the music I had borrowed from the beginning. Now I am the toast of a town where silver crosses the palms that mesmerize the new kids who can barely cross the street without losing an inch off their lives. The nasty redhead who lived by my side is gone, but I am still here, groaning by the pool while I recycle the twelve notes I have written to myself.

I am good natured to the max, a stabilizing influence on those who fall apart. I am a toy and a joke, but indispensable to the cause. Without me, there is nothing, because I am good and kind; but be warned that if pushed too far I will withdraw what the world cannot live without. I have found myself on the twelfth step, looking down and around at all of the show business I never dreamed would be my life to pretend. And now, good friends, I twist my girded wrists and turn my concave back with humilty and trust for I know my modesty becomes you all.

I am terrified of the grotesque embodiments projected by my own vision of self. The fear and hatred and love that flooded the vacuum left by those who did not care, built up in me like a tsunami poised to conquer the earth for all time. And it happened, but not for all time and not for all people. And it brought back no one who was gone, and it left in its wake those I was meant to love but could not. I became shiftless and cruel, and entitled to all I was given and could take. How I was born into fame as a part of a whole was then meaningless to me and the one whose aggression became my heart. My music was no longer music, but something else, desperate and cold. It lived to prove it could live on its own but it could not. I was beholden to my better halves who were not better and who proved it to me beyond a shadowed doubt. I saved the world many times over and became a prophet for desperate and dangerous times. All weekends were lost and I fell with tragic company.

It's just so blue to be alive in this skin and standing on a rock where only the trees can see and my only true friend blackens my lungs and ruins my voice. To be a child and to have a child are not the same thing and to be free and to be protected by those who aren't afraid but will sacrifice your true artistry to the coin of a realm, where all is as it seems not to be, is more than I can sometimes stand. I am a soulful curmudgeon in a coat of many colours that bleed into the heart of who I am and who no one understands; not even the mother of us all who stands and waits for the beloved interval of blessed freedom. Of all the phonies pretending their phony art you of all people should know the real breadth of how I feel and how I yearn for the dead to come alive.

When your yin is a yang, that's a wacky two thumbs in the air that have to come down. But we'll carry on, even though a world of resentment seeps through the pores of my innate cheer. How could one who used every advantage to appear to come out on top, even though there was nothing that could ever replace what was gone from the first, leave me alone to repair a legacy that wasn't there. I put my hurt aside like a dead string and go where I'm wanted, which is everywhere. But there's always something missing that I cannot feel. I use the best I can find, and pay them the respect they don't deserve, and they know it. I will play this game til they tear the clothes from my back and send me harking to the home of the brave.

It's cold in the abbey and it's colder in the alley where the raccoons pester my heart and tear at the chits stained with the blood of your sin. To work a soul that has suffered for belief when no belief was necessary and all but the heart lingered in the cathedral of the profane to see and to feel the agony of disillusionment printed in the court of despair is brutal to the core. I must be among your number to be counted when no numbers are to be found and only family gather to give props to the cold flights to oblivion I must take again and again. But your sweet eyes are always there, glistening with delight as I reckon the strange cost of familiarity and the delicious end game we must play while the wheeling generals fire across the bows of empty admirals diseased in the steaming bay of pigs. My fascination with the war will end someday and all will breathe their last as only I remain forever yours in the golden blast of never.

WILD AWAKE

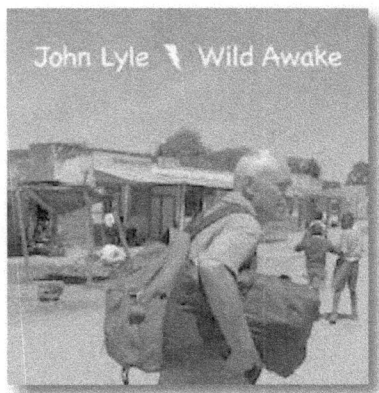

2010

I wrote my first song on the piano when I was fifteen. It was called *Cold Grapes From a Blue Bowl* and was inspired by a movie I'd seen on tv, starring John Hodiak as a gangster who had risen from poverty by virtue of his violence and to whom elegance and stature were symbolized by cold grapes from a blue bowl. He got the house on the hill, the cars, the beautiful wife, the grapes from the bowl and the electric chair.

ABOVE THE RAIN

Above the rain like a child against a broken window pane
All the lines in a nursery rhyme can't find that time again
Nothing like the dawn to brighten your day
Wave her magic wand her magical way

Above the rain like a weathervane, with nowhere to turn
Folding grass don't know to ask gods for air to burn
Nothing like the dawn to brighten your day
Wave her magic wand her magical way

Above the rain, like a man insane, upon a fiery steed
Frozen hooves destroy the roofs above what lies beneath
Nothing like the dawn to brighten your day
Wave her magic wand her magical way

Above the rain, on another plane, you can see everything's alright
The sky is blue and the wind blows through ribbons of pure light
Nothing like the dawn to brighten your day
Wave her magic wand her magical way
Over and over and over and over again

I THOUGHT I SAW YOU

I thought I saw you where the weeping willows grow
Down by the river wearing someone else's clothes
Then the wind did change and softly touch my brow
As if to say, I am with you now

But when I looked again you were no longer there
Not but a shadow held my world of stormy care
I'd sworn remembrance soon forgotten with the day
Everything appears to pass away

I thought I saw you but my seeing was in vain
When all I wanted was to see you once again
I thought I saw you where the hills of evening glow
You were wearing someone else's clothes

HOLD ON AS SHE GOES

Outside The Golden Lantern hoboes wear no clothes
They set a certain standard I'm gonna go below
Look at the faceless wonder blowing through the rye
Tripping 'cross the tundra, thrilling to the sky

The pouring rain keeps saying hold on as she goes
There's no time to waste in this holy place
Hold on as she goes

The milk of human kindness warming in the sun
How better to remind us, nothing will be done

The pouring rain keeps saying hold on as she goes
There's no time to waste in this holy place
Hold on as she goes

Outside The Golden Lantern the fires have gone cold
The homeless search the ashes for the things they've been told

The pouring rain keeps saying hold on as she goes
There's no time to waste in this holy place
Hold on as she goes

THEY STONED HER

She wore the scarlet letter like a chain
Across the wellspring of her heart
Those who knew no better turned their backs
And stole the rocks from her hearth

They stoned her in the foothills where she'd left the chosen path
They stoned her with her buried up unto the neck in sand
These are the twisted teachings from the ancient, ragged throat
Of a misbegotten shadow from the nightmare of a goat

In the lonesome valley broken blossoms scent the morning air
No one builds a coffin while a child is held aloft to stare

They stoned her in the foothills where she'd left the chosen path
They stoned her with her buried up unto the neck in sand
These are the twisted teachings from the ancient, ragged throat
Of a misbegotten shadow from the nightmare of a goat

SHADOW OF THE WASTELAND

In the shadow of the wasteland in the desert of the heart
All the threads have come unravelled, all the dogs have lost their bark
In the shadow of the wasteland where the heathen start to pray
Like the rain must fall, they'll be leavin' there someday

In the shadow of the wasteland they're buried where they stand
Trying to get heaven in a strange and distant land
In the shadow of the wasteland there ain't nothin' left to say
Like the rain must fall, they'll be leavin' there someday

They got the motor runnin' but they have nowhere to go
They hear the cattle lowin' but they got no horn to blow

In the shadow of the wasteland in the desert of the heart
Something's always coming and it's always off the chart
In the shadow of the wasteland there ain't nothin' left to say
Like the rain must fall, they'll be leavin' there someday

A NEW BANDANA

Cut-throat morons with their bloody horns and their bodies
  made of beer
Oh Susanna, got a new bandana but I won't wear it here
There's a place where the shining face of freedom takes a stand
Whosoever's gonna hold together way down in Neverland

You start out golden then you wind up holding
All the things your mother told you
You had to know to get to go, where it is you'll never know
The sacrifice you'll have to make to find your calling
Oh so many tears keep falling

Screw repentance, it's a whole life sentence and that's a lot of years
Oh Susanna, got a new bandana but I won't wear it here
There's a place where the shining face of freedom takes a stand
Whosoever's gonna hold together way down in Never
Down in Never, down in Never, down in Never, down
  in Neverland

I felt much better when I wrote that letter 'bout the moonshadow
And the old ladder, and the silver that fell from your hair
I felt so shattered when it still mattered I'm too cold to care
Screw repentance, it's a whole life sentence and that's a lot of years
Oh Susanna, got a new bandana but I won't wear it here

There's a place where the shining face
Of freedom takes a stand
Whosoever's gonna hold together
Way down in Never, down in Never, down in Never
Down in Never, down in Never, down in Never, down
  in Neverland

No One Knows

No one knows where minutes go to while away the hours
No one knows they find repose in shadows of the flowers
Down the road where no one knows the twists and turns abide
You and me go flyin' free on wings of butterflies

No one knows how tender shows of colour touch the heart
No one knows the dying throes of winter like the lark
Down the road where no one knows the twists and turns abide
You and me go flyin' free on wings of butterflies

No one knows and so it goes, the staggered poets chime
No one knows the plight of those who live their lives in time
Down the road where no one knows the twists and turns abide
You and me go flyin' free on wings of butterflies

LOVE IS

Love is hot, love is cold
Love will still be in our hearts
When we've grown old

If you'll take my hand, we'll go on making plans
Til we both understand love anew

Love is me, love is you
Love is still the only system that'll do

If you'll take my hand we'll go on making plans
Til we both understand love anew

Many's the couple get into trouble driven apart by their pride
Loving is giving and only by giving can loving be made to survive

Love goes out, loves comes in
Love is true and what we've really always been

If you'll take my hand we'll go on making plans
Til we both understand love anew

ANOTHER GOLDEN DREAM

All my roses refuse to tantalize
They ain't for tellin' no more lies
No striking poses
Where the red dirt road divides
Ain't no need for no disguise

Who lights a candle
When the moon is on the rise
Where is the fortress for my pride
Another golden dream has set upon this town
Who builds a house to burn it down

Any number trust the winds of change
Holy freedom in a cage
All asunder, scattered to the age
Falling down into a rage

Who lights a candle
When the moon is on the rise
Where is the fortress for my pride
Another golden dream has set upon this town
Who builds a house to burn it down

THE MOURNING DOVE

Was a mourning dove in the old grey window
I heard his song, I don't know when though
For my eyes did cloud with unknown sorrows
That had blinded me to the day

Was a mourning dove on the highest rafter
The heartless spoke their final answer
To the waiting crowd whose moment shattered
Into pieces cold as the clay

It's a rising up and laying down
Of a boundless love and thorny crown
It's a rising up and laying down

Was a mourning dove in the sweet hereafter
Who sang his song of joy and laughter
With an endless heart where it's all looked after
And the rolling sky's never grey

It's a rising up and laying down
Of a boundless love and thorny crown
It's a rising up and laying down

The lyrics for this song co-written with Bob Bradshaw.

THE WALLS OF JERICHO

Sunbeams echo through the twilight of time
Broken shadows come and render us blind
Can't read the writing on the walls of Jericho

Phantom thieves with no eyes of delight
Bare their arms in the house of blue lights
That's what you get inside the walls of Jericho

Out on borrowed air the crooked bay moons
Ammunition for the crack of the runes
Thrown again against the walls of Jericho

What can be hides behind the night
Like a rope of sand, it just can't stand the light

Fingerprints on the mirror of the mind
Wash away with the tears of the tide
Still and gone beside the walls of Jericho

OPEN WIDE

Against the drift of reason
There appeared another season
Darkness could not hide
All that had closed was open wide

Shifting like the weather
With the fortunes of a feather
Much to my surprise
All that had closed was open wide

Always loosely woven
When a pledge from the beholden
Need not be denied
All that had closed was open wide

Wholly out of balance
Like the wonderland of Alice
Outside battle lines
All that had closed was open wide

I KNOW WHO I AM

I know who I am, I know why I'm here
I know who I am, now I understand
What was far is near

You can take my eyes, you can take my ears
You can take my heart but the loving part
Will not disappear

Is it any wonder how clear the truth can be
Was I expecting thunder and lightning to set me free

You have searched the sky, you have searched the sea
You can search the sands for a thousand lands
But you won't find me

Is it any wonder how clear the truth can be
Was I expecting thunder and lightning to help me see

I am that which drives this body
I am that which made it be
And I will break it down
And wash it to the sea

KNOWN CORNERS

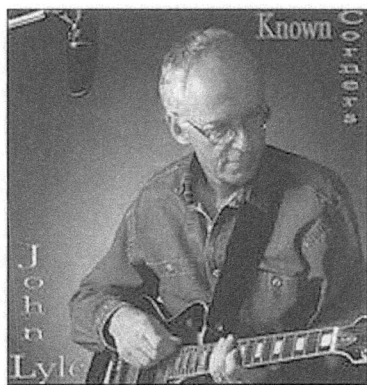

2007

I got to know Paul Rodgers a little bit. My day job for twenty-nine years was being a postman. Paul moved onto my route because he'd fallen in love with the lady who lived there. He came out one day and I introduced myself. I said I was a songwriter and he said sarcastically 'we're all songwriters, mate!' I said, no, I really am and I'm good and I've got some stuff you could sing the hell out of! That took him aback, and he said to leave a cd in the mailbox which I did. Months went by and I forgot about it. Then he came out and I just kept going because I thought he'd blown me off and was the typical unreliable musician, compounded by celebrity paranoia, which he might suffer from. He chased me down the street, said he'd listened to the stuff and loved it, wondered if I still performed. It was great. He was really down to earth and just another guy. Then he disappeared again, as did I. The 'lead' track I gave him was 'I Need Another Kiss', a soulful r&b track from *Almost Like Fate*. (Available on iTunes as is most every song in this book!)

We All Fall Down

You were sitting by a river
Lost inside of days gone by
Something came and made you shiver
Something came and made you cry

How much would you beg or borrow
For it to be the way it was
Would you pay the wage of sorrow
Pretty is as pretty does

Life's a bed of roses
Where the magic comes and grows
Hushabye, we all fall down
Humbled as we tumble
Over ruins that have crumbled
Hushabye, without a sound

Did you see your Mother's image
Painted in a pale, blue sky
Did you see the Painter in it
Clean a brush in tears you cry

Life's a bed of roses
Where the magic comes and grows
Hushabye, we all fall down
Humbled as we tumble
Over ruins that have crumbled
Hushabye, without a sound

BONE DRY

Someone said that you have gone bone dry
There is not a thing can make you cry
You can sail a painted ship across a silver sea
And bring it home without a thought of me

Up all night, waiting for the rain
I might have to dance that dance again
Shake my fist into the sun
And beat my feet across
The barren face of everything I've lost

Whosoever built this paradise
Forgot to put the light behind your eyes
You can sail a painted ship across a silver sea
And bring it home without a thought of me

If I live to see the light of dawn
I hope that when I wake you will be gone
Then I will slip my painted feet
Into my painted shoes
And walk away, bone dry just like you
Walk away, bone dry just like you

I KNOW YOU RIDER

Could be a story or it could be true
Could be about me, it could be about you
I've lost so many reasons for things I think I've done
If I thought this pride of fools
Called the shots and made the rules
I'd take a flying leap back to the place from where I came
I know you, rider, but I love you just the same

You've been trying to break a code
You've been trying to drop a load
You've been carrying your own mountain
Past the point of no return
You've been living where the sun goes down
Where what goes around, comes around
They say a storm is brewing but they won't give it a name
I know you, rider, but I love you just the same

Waves are lapping like a big dog's tongue
Just like it happened back when we were young
You're not here to solve the problems of the world
Standing on the corner with your wings pinned back
Barefoot and pregnant on a mountain path
Screaming to the heavens like a keeper of the flame

I know you, rider, but I love you just the same
I know you, rider, like a dreamer knows his hand
Like a rose that grows you'll come to know I'm your biggest fan

In the velvet afterglow of memory I go
Footloose and funny in the shadow of the show
I hear you whisper there ain't no wind at all
You made it here without a map
All the stars smile behind your back
You tremble at the mention of
The One who has no name
I know you, rider, but I love you just the same

BOUND AND DETERMINED

I must have missed it
Cause you sure had it ready to go
You had it all sewed up
Like a head on the wall for show
Your ducks were all in line
You must have went to Columbine

Bound and determined
You will keep what you have not got

Is that a purse you hold so close
To your cardboard heart
I try to stand still
When your dead eye begins to dart
The crowd down on Slaughter Row
They'll watch a child see the red blood flow

Bound and determined
You will keep what you have not got

You take it so personal
Like it's something you think you own
Something to hide behind when you get back home
No, no, no, no!

Funny, Funny Animal

You're a funny funny animal,
But I forgot to laugh
They think you're together
But you're cut right in half

I see you prowlin', like a god of the dead
I hear you howlin' like a wind in the head

You're a funny funny animal
Pretending to be kind
All the while, you been double-dealin' from behind

I see you prowlin', like a god of the dead
I hear you howlin' like a wind in the head

With a begging bowl in one hand
And a knife behind your back
You hide like a jackal
With some kittens in a sack

I see you prowlin', like a god of the dead
I hear you howlin' like a wind in the head

You're a funny funny animal
Loathsome to yourself
Dirty, and unwanted, but you can't be no one else

A BREATH OF LIGHT

Love lies bleeding, in the death of night
Something needs a breath of light
Birds are feeding, they are hoarding for a flight
To where the wild things lose their sight

Tribal drums are beating rhythm out of time
What it is, is not mine
Just missed meeting a meeting of the minds
Being half a double bind

A lonesome wind-chime beating on itself
Like a hollow, empty shell
Not even this time, could there be any help
That's all she wrote that I can tell

All the boulders standing in the way
Have turned to dust and blown away
Both the shoulders they cried on every day
Have grown wings and flown away

We fly so slow and low we almost touch the ground
With laughing children all around
It's always touch and go on the borderline
With so many ways to be kind

For Kerrie Speers.

LIKE A BLANK

My guts are tied in knots my eyes are filled with clay
I'll get there when I leave when I get my way
Like a blank I missed it
Guess I better roll it back one more time

Branded like a long horn on the down hill drag
Drunk on my reflection like an evening stag
Like a blank I missed it
Guess I must have had a hole in my mind

There's a fire on the mountain, there's a fire below
There's a fire in the garden where the wind won't blow
Like a blank I missed it
Guess I better roll it back one more time

I guess I better roll it back like a big old stone
Nothin' gonna stop it on its way back home
Like a blank I missed it
Guess I better roll it back one more time

Like a blank I missed it
Guess I better roll it back one more time
I better roll it back down the railroad track
There ain't nothin' at the end of the line

There's a fire on the mountain. there's a fire below
There's a fire in the garden where the wind won't blow
Like a blank I missed it
Guess I better roll it back one more time

CITY OF LOVE

In the city of love, the cops don't use a gun
They catch you with the stars in your eyes
The sun don't shine, it radiates
The mystery train is never late
Clouds don't hold no rain in the city of love
Clouds don't hold no rain in the city of love

In the city of love, all change comes from above
Singing like a stone in the sea
We stand and pray for who knows what
But every case is open shut
Clouds don't hold no rain in the city of love
Clouds don't hold no rain in the city of love

In the city of love, I'm glad for what I got
Flashing like a bolt from the blue
Shining as my own true face
Laughing down this bitter place
Clouds don't hold no rain in the city of love
Clouds don't hold no rain in the city of love

In the city of love, I dreamt I never was
Drifting like a ghost in the wind
Backing down a faded stair
Past a clock I can't repair
Clouds don't hold no rain in the city of love
Clouds don't hold no rain in the city of love

♪ COOL FIRE

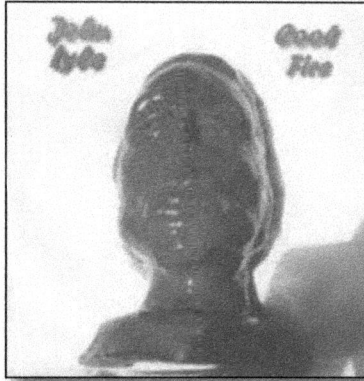

2005

In 1972, I auditioned for the Mariposa Folk Festival which was held on a small island near Toronto. I didn't get the gig but I was given a performer's pass. I rode over on the ferry with Joni Mitchell, Jackson Browne and the ferry boat operator. Joni and Jackson were fighting so Joni came over and sat beside me. She didn't say a word and I wasn't going to be the first to speak so nobody did. She put on lipstick, which shattered my illusions.

WHEN THE WIND GETS HIGH

The carousel is finally winding down
They've pulled up stakes
And scraped the makeup off the clown
Not even time can mend this broken-hearted town

I would run away and quit the circus now
If I could overcome the things that make me proud
I would stand so tall my head would be a cloud

I've been counting backward in my sleep
Breaking down the horror of belief
I've been laughing at things that give me grief

I'm gonna shave my head
And put my hat on backward:
They say that works
When the wind gets high

You and me, we're lost inside a bud
Dizzy with a fever in the blood
Let me close my eyes
And sink into the flood

My old red rooster crows at dawn
When everything I've prayed against is gone
He leans his back against the fence
And sings a song

I'm gonna shave my head
And put my hat on backwards
They say that works
When the wind gets high

WALK IT ON DOWN

Scientologists are coming, there's a Mormon at the door
There's a Witness counting heads but he don't know what for

The glory train has left the track, it's barrelling down the street
Scaring the bejesus out of everyone it meets

Walk it on down, walk it on down
Walk it on down to the best guy in town

The sound of distant thunder makes him dream about his past
Just how many blunders can one guy amass?

He searches for his Bible in the rushes, sweet and low
A desperate guy is liable to find anywhere to go

Walk it on down, walk it on down
Walk it on down to the best guy in town

If I told you the dye was cast you'd laugh into my face
You'd write my name upon the wind and turn another page

The book of life is filled with lies claiming to be true
I'll bet you any money the biggest lie is you

Walk it on down, walk it on down
Walk it on down to the best guy in town

A Dog Lies Down Sometime

You scream around the corner, like Little Jack Horner
Who knows what's down the line?
It's a stone-cold fact, they'll be bringing you back
In a box of yellow pine

We all have our moments, but yours takes an hour
If it does not take a day
I'd cut you some slack, but it's down the track
Where my best intentions stay

Meet your maker, he's an undertaker
With an old Econoline
He's got a black pomade, a Tibetan maid,
And he loves his life of crime

You run around in circles like a dog in a circus
But a dog lies down sometime
If you swear at the moon and it breaks in two
You can take it as a sign

Scrape the haggis off the wall at the lesbians' ball
Take your big foot off my throat
Write a letter to the Pope, we gotta legalize dope
And don't forget to vote

Meet your maker, he's an old heart-breaker
With his own line of clothes
He's got a straw-bale shack, by the railroad track
And he breathes through his nose

You run around in circles like a dog in a circus
But a dog lies down sometime
If you swear at the moon and it breaks in two
You can take it as a sign

🎼 DO WHALES HAVE SCALES

Do whales have scales? Do they go 'do ^{re} ^{me'} for so long,
Or, are they the avante coast guard? Do they go 'do _{re} _{me}'?

Do whales tell tales? Do they meet and sound and then go 'round
To Namu's bar and shoot the bull, until the cows come home?

Do whales feel frail? Do they start to blubber like a real
land-lubber.
When they think about the journey's end, then, do they get
the bends?

Of the many mammals in history, could there be one
smarter than me?
Was it shrewd for whales to conclude they'd be better off
back in the sea?

I wanna know!

Will whales prevail? Will they grow immune to our harpoons
And live to learn to be like us, awfully omnivorous?

Of the many mammals in history, could there be one
smarter than me?
Was it shrewd for whales to conclude, was it wise for whales
to surmise,
Was it bright for whales to think they might be better off
back in the sea?

I'm gonna find out

TOO MUCH COMPASSION

The biggest bully in the yard
Could always put me off my guard
By pulling out a hanky with his hand
This guy's not half so bad, he's got a cold just like I had
And some sisters, and a mother with a womb

Then he'd turn into a viper, and I'd wish I'd stayed hyper
As a seismograph about to overload
Lift the veil of paranoia and the devil's damn destroyers
Zero in and aim to blow me off the globe

Too much compassion can kill a nervous man
And too much pity's bound to drown him on dry land
Tender-hearted heartlessness is how it all began
It takes two to tangle in this cock-eyed caravan

Trillions of gifts beneath the tree
And there was only one for me
Just a cap gun, but it really rang the bell
I'd wanted it like sin, since my last pistol'd packed it in
Brand new, it bit the dust, and rusted in the rain

Then somebody said, aw, honey,
We just could not find the money to give you your due
That broke me up inside
Drop the veil of paranoia, and the devil's damn destroyers
Zero in and aim to blow me off the globe

Too much compassion can kill a nervous man
And too much pity's bound to drown him on dry land
Tender-hearted heartlessness is how it all began
It takes two to tangle in this cock-eyed caravan

BLIND LOVE

Evil forces gather in the half-light
Dark with blood, but only in the mind
In the cold desert bloom
There's nothing left but room
For pride in knowing love is blind

Tongues so thick,
They cannot speak of weather
Bodies ache, with things they have not done
To see what is true, and have to live it too
Is a fate that should not befall anyone

I've lived most of my life paralyzed
Pretending I can see
When I've been looking through
The wrong set of eyes
When I can just let go
Like an angel in the snow
I'll be the King of the Cowboys
On this sweet little pony of mine

OLD HONTANA ROAD

Inga said a mouthful when she said
I could get her back after she's dead
You should hear what people say
About her now she's gone
But I will take the high road from now on

Rain comes down like bullets from above
Money can't buy this kind of love

Some old twister, spinning like a top
The way he moves, you think he'll never stop
Just when you think you know someone
You find out they're like you
Living in a room without a view

Sun burns down on Old Hontana Road
Turn your head, and you won't see them go
You won't see scarecrows smile
At nothing in the dirt
You won't see them leave a world of hurt

I WON'T BE LONESOME WHEN I'M GONE

I may have been in China
When you came to break the news
Trying to give me something I can use
I remember kind of peeling back into my blues
Fetching for a pail to fill my shoes

All graven images, from sea to shining sea
Another smiling Christ, smiling back at me
Woke up this morning with a hammer and a tong
I won't be lonesome when I'm gone

I'm gonna backslide 'til I find an open door
Backslide 'til I can't backslide no more
Every cold idea that thinks it knows the score
Don't seem to mean so much no more

It must have been a foggy night, when you fell for me
Everything you could forget, you managed not to see
Woke up this morning with a hammer and a tong
I won't be lonesome when I'm gone

One hand on the shovel, one foot in the grave
Watch another breath go down the drain
If you see my double, ask him if he has a name
And if he's taking rest inside the shade

Everything you love in me, you hide inside yourself
Turn it outside over, you don't need no one's help
Woke up this morning with a hammer and a tong
I won't be lonesome when I'm gone

SPARKLING RIVER

Like a faded leaf, hanging by a thread
I blow into the wind and tumble down like I was dead
I say I'm not a thief but I won't stand in the light
So you can wash my face and give my empty mouth a bite

How can I be angry with someone so nice
Are my fingers made of silver, is my heart made of ice?
I hide beside the fire with tears in my eyes
Mourning the desire I've learned to despise

You know where I'm going, you know where I've been
You know which wind's blowing and you know it's not a sin

You make a good sheepdog moving me along
All tangled up in what don't last long
On the outskirts of the meadow, in the shadow of fright
Crazy wolves are mending fences in the starry, starry night

You know where I'm going, you know where I've been
You know which wind's blowing and you know it's not a sin

There is a sparkling river flowing through my head
Bringing understanding who I thought I was is dead
Rollin' and 'a tumblin,' through wind, and stone and sea
Laughing like a baby when a baby is free

♪ DOWN THE ROAD AND FAR AWAY

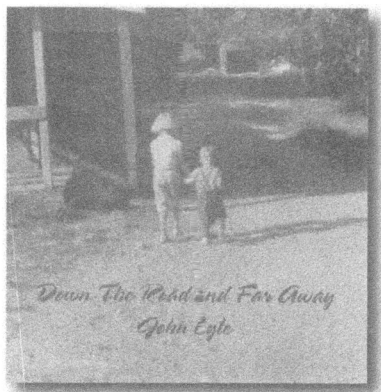

Down The Road and Far Away
John Eyle

2002

Jessie Colin Young was a big influence vocally. I saw him whenever I could in the 60s and early 70's and made a point of meeting him and trying to sell him some songs, which I thought he needed. I went backstage after a concert and asked a woman who was going into the green room if she would ask Jesse if he could come out because I had some songs for him. She said, *'I think I can do that, I'm his wife.'* I waited and I waited, and then a guy I knew came along, said hi and walked into the room like he owned it. I waited for what seemed like hours until Jesse's wife came along again from the same direction she'd come from in the first place. She said, *'are you still holding up this wall?'* I said, *'uh huh.'* Dark clouds appeared in her lovely eyes and she stormed into the green room. Jesse was out in thirty seconds flat. I don't know what he was on, but he was on something. His eyes were like dead marbles but he was gracious and coherent and full of cautionary tales about the music business. He took my tape of thirty songs and disappeared like Paul Rodgers.

JUST MY KIND OF GIRL

I asked her what she did for fun, she said she didn't know
She said the days seemed shorter now love had lost its glow
She said all her bags were packed and waiting on the bed
And if I thought I had a chance I'd better shake my head

She said complete removal was quite beyond the pale
She had to stick around a while until she saved the whales
She had to stick around until she made me see the light
All my ideals are only clouding up my sight

Ain't no doubt about it, she's just my kind of girl
Too bad she lives so far away
She's half asleep and far too deep into this crazy world
Ain't no doubt about it, she's just my kind of girl

She said she'd given up on hope and all that it implied
She looked at me and said I see sadness in your eyes
She said when you stop arguing with what has to be
You'll learn the only lesson you'll ever learn from me

Ain't no doubt about it, she's just my kind of girl
Too bad she lives so far away
She's half asleep and far too deep into this crazy world
Ain't no doubt about it, she's just my kind of girl

I got a funny feeling we met somewhere before
Maybe in a focus group the year before the war
You had a red bandana wrapped around your pretty neck
I would have loved you way back then but someone stacked the deck

Ain't no doubt about it, she's just my kind of girl
Too bad she lives so far away
She's half asleep and far too deep into this crazy world
Ain't no doubt about it, she's just my kind of girl

OLD JOE CALLS FROM THE HILL

Old Joe calls from the hill
To the boy standing alone
Old man drunk by the still
Don't know nothing he's done

Momma in the kitchen
Cuts you with her tongue
Old Joe calls from the hill
To the boy standing alone

Hair yellow as straw
Eyes blue as the grass
Heart lone as the pine
But it don't know what to ask

Somewhere from the hill
Old Joe's plaintive moan
Drifts upon the wind
To the boy standing alone

Lyrics for this song co-written with Penny Lyle.

MY LOVE IS EVERYTHING

Clean and pure as a mountain stream
Dignified as a college dean
Alive as life has ever been
My love is everything to me

My love is everything she can be
My love is everything to me
My love is everything
Dancing in the heart and mind
Of everybody she can find

Reaching to the heavens
Probing inner space
My love is touch and sight and sound
And always in good taste

Yet one thing can defeat her
And bring her to her knees
And force her from my memory
Like the moon removes the sea

But what care I for Father Time
He too is growing old
And at least for now, I am warm
While he is always cold

CENTERS

I'll bet nothing can get so small
It can't be cut in two
And I'll bet nothing can be bigger
Than what's inside of you

I'll bet it all goes on forever
Not just outwardly, but in
I'll bet we're each of us a center
And that's what we've always been

So if you're feeling out of things
Lonely tired and blue
Remember you're a center
And there's centers all 'round you

LITTLE KNIVES

I'm tired unto death from all these little knives
It's not the big one that gets you
It's when they come in fives
I don't know what I want but I know I want it now

The snow lies heavy on the powerline tonight
I don't know where I find the strength to hold you tight
Maybe it's the same place I finally come to see

All the contradictions holding me down
Ain't nothing but the chatter from a brain-dead clown
Ain't nothing but the chains I'm dragging to my grave

Don't the rain sound lovely hiding in the air
I tried to cross my heart and say it wasn't there
Help me tie my shoe and point me to the stair

I need to be deliberate in everything I do
I'm being left behind by everyone but you
I want to go so slow I get behind my mind

If I could see through this illusion I wouldn't say a word
I wouldn't try to argue what we both know is absurd
I wouldn't lift a finger in anger or in trust

THE CAMEL'S BACK

If you're disappointed, the old man said to me
It's 'cause you expected what was not to be
That's when I shot him and as he went to hell
I said remember you're my major disappointment number twelve

Disappointment number twelve didn't break the camel's back
I'd guacamole for a camel
If a camel had the knack, I'd climb upon its back
I'd ride into the desert 'til the desert starts to crack
Righteous anger burns the sea, floods the land and calls to me
Kill the moon and blind the sun until the revolution's done

I was feelin' like a mountain climber lost inside the Alps
When she came between twin heartbeats and said she needed help
That's when I unloaded, and as she met her fate
I said, remember you're my major disappointment number eight

Disappointment number eight didn't break the camel's back
I'd guacamole for a camel
If a camel had the knack, I'd climb upon its back
I'd ride into the desert 'til the desert starts to crack
Righteous anger burns the sea, floods the land and calls to me
Kill the moon and blind the sun until the revolution's done

I was telling these stories to another friend of mine
When he came up with this classic line
Don't that gavel get heavy? I said let me be the judge of that
And you're the worst disappointment I ever had

Disappointments that I had didn't break the camel's back
I'd guacamole for a camel
If a camel had the knack, I'd climb upon its back
I'd ride into the desert 'til the desert starts to crack
Righteous anger burns the sea, floods the land and calls to me
Kill the moon and blind the sun until the revolution's done

HIGUEY HAIRCUT

Higuey haircut's mighty fine
Takes a bite out of my mind, my mind
Barber, help me travel light
When I take my homeward flight, tonight

Broken pavement tricks my feet
Sunshine burns the hanging meat, the meat
Sugar coffee don't do squat
Por favor, another shot, make it hot

Tim can rollers on her head
Clank upon her marble bed, the bed
Power and water come and go
But nothing stops the passing show, the show

Hot merengue fills my ear
Time to have an otra beer
An otra beer, over here

Ay carumba, she can't do the rhumba
She might have a bug
Chills and fever, will they ever leave her
She might have to take a drug

Lyrics for this song co-written with Penny Lyle.

WAY PAST NOW

Way past now, past the burning cow
Where the salesmen never stop
Where the road rolls deep
And keening sheep sacrifice their crop

Noble steeds have lost their feed
While Agnes chews her mop
Way past now, space and time have wowed
But no one calls the cops

I'm feeling helpless, Agnes
And a little reckless too
Take me down your garden path
And I will go with you

Way past now past the trampled vows
And the pleasure that is cruel
Some old man with an empty hand
Speaks the language of a fool

I just listen to my teardrops glisten
As they slide into the sand
I'm too tired to fall asleep
But I'll do what I can

I'm feeling helpless, Agnes
And a little reckless too
Take me down your garden path
And I will go with you

TOO LATE TO PANIC

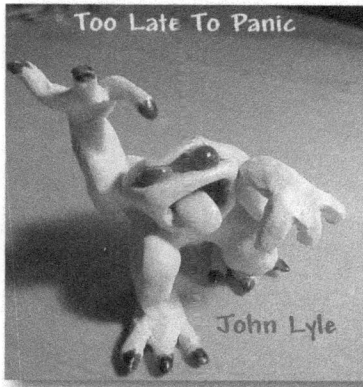

Too Late To Panic

John Lyle

2000

The first person I noticed when I got onto the island of Mariposa in 1972 was Bob Dylan. He asked someone if he knew when Leon Redbone was going to play. I wandered off to to a quiet spot and leaned against a fence. Dylan came along by himself and walked up to me. We stood and looked at each other for a few minutes until we both left. I walked around for a while and then climbed a hill to get an overview of the scene. Then I saw what looked like a snake winding its way through the grounds and for a minute I couldn't understand what it was. Dylan had been discovered and everywhere he went a single file line of fans followed. There were hundreds of people in that line; it was as if they were lining up at a book signing but the author had his back turned and was looking for Leon Redbone.

HOPE SIGNALS

I am not an Indian from two hundred years ago
I don't live in a teepee, and I can't shoot a bow
I'm out of touch with nature, and I watch too much tv
But I hope, when I die, there'll be another me

I'm sending hope signals across the Great Divide
Hope signals, send me back in time
I want to be an Indian out on the Western Plain
Come a-ty-yi-yipee
Come a-ty-yi-yipee-yipee-yay

I'll be a Shawnee buck with braids in my hair
I'll drink the sparkling water and I'll breathe the living air
I'll love a tender maiden underneath the shining stars
And I'll never have to ride in the beast they call the car

I'm sending hope signals across the Great Divide
Hope signals, send me back in time
I want to be an Indian out on the Western Plain
Come a-ty-yi-yipee
Come a-ty-yi-yipee-yipee-yay

The coyote will howl at the fullness of the moon
With an aching in his heart, like a frost on love in bloom
And when the Europeans with their rifles and their booze
Come and show me how to win,
I will show them how to lose

I'm sending hope signals across the Great Divide
Hope signals, send me back in time
I want to be an Indian out on the Western Plain
Come a-ty-yi-yipee
Come a-ty-yi-yipee-yipee-yay

A LITTLE BIT OF HEAVEN ON A SATURDAY NIGHT

Job had some issues he couldn't comprehend
God had principles He wasn't gonna bend
Christ was on a mission that was coming to an end
Satan was the wild card masquerading as a friend

A little bit of heaven on a Saturday night
As long as we're still here we're gonna feel alright
A little bit of heaven on a Saturday night
When the sun comes up, I'm gonna shoot out the lights

I work very, very hard and I'm very, very bright
If I need a little on the side I think you might
Look the other way and take a pill
All us good ol' boys you know we do what we will

A little bit of heaven on a Saturday night
As long as we're still here we're gonna feel alright
A little bit of heaven on a Saturday night
When the sun comes up, I'm gonna shoot out the lights

My daddy was a drunkard and my momma was a whore
If I thought you could take it, I'd tell you some more
It takes a double shot of love to fill the emptiness inside
Let him stand and judge who has not lied

A little bit of heaven on a Saturday night
As long as we're still here we're gonna feel alright
A little bit of heaven on a Saturday night
When the sun comes up, I'm gonna shoot out the lights

TURN YOUR LAMP DOWN, MOMMA

There's a mine in the hill
Every night she moans and groans
There's a mine in the hill
Every night she moans and groans
She says nobody wants me
They think I'm made of stone

The old prospector he just passes by
The old prospector he just passes by
He says listen, pretty momma,
I got bigger fish to fry

Got a letter this mornin' postmarked Cinnamon Wells
Got a letter this mornin' postmarked Cinnamon Wells
Edged in black and full of living cells

Turn your lamp down, momma, your daddy's comin' home
Turn your lamp down, momma, your daddy's comin' home
You been too long lonely and I been too long gone

EARTH TO MOTHER

Earth to Mother, here's a message from me
What's it like up there in Heaven
Do you watch tv?
Do they let you bounce God's children
On your lovely little knee?
Earth to Mother, here's a message from me

Earth to Mother, are you making any friends?
It's not easy being the new kid, trying so hard to blend
Trying to muster up the courage to start over again
Earth to Mother, how long has it been?

Earth to Mother, rest your tired eyes
Put your feet up on a cloud and let it roll by
Everybody loves you, especially me
Earth to Mother, you're finally free

Earth to Mother, I must sign off
I promised myself a round of golf
If I'm ever in your neighbourhood
You know I'll drop by
Earth to Mother, of course, that's after I die

IN THE WRECKAGE OF OUR LOVE

In the wreckage of our love the black box can't be found
Experts search for clues while the neighbours gather around
They're havin' themselves a party
While the good time's goin' down

The twisted fuselage hides the pieces of my heart
I tried to keep it all together, but I was doomed from the start
But you can't blame a guy for trying to light a fire in the dark

Angel on my shoulder says 'I think I'm getting colder
Won't you go and get me a shawl?'
Heavenly chorus say they'll chip in for the florist
'If you'll only make sense of it all'

Black smoke fills the sky while reporters take my name
I must remind myself it's only just a game
But next time, baby, we better take the train

LONESOME DADDY BLUES

Every day of the week might as well be blue Monday
Every pot of gold might as well be a barrel of rain
Every sunbeam might as well be a shadow, until you're
    in my arms again

You're seeing in me what you found in him
But I ain't guilty of nothin' but being your friend
I'm like a pauper at the wrong end of the rainbow
With those lonesome daddy blues

Every smile might as well be a death mask
Every ribbon might as well be a chain
Every tomorrow might as well be yesterday until you're
    in my arms again

You're seeing in me what you found in him
But I ain't guilty of nothin', but being your friend
I'm like a pauper at the wrong end of the rainbow
With those lonesome daddy blues

Got the lonesome daddy blues,
From the top of my head to the bottom of my shoes
Got the lonesome daddy blues
Have some, buddy, I got more than I can use

𝄞 PAY ME NO MIND

I met her on the internet, we chatted through the night
I was off my medication, so I took the next flight
She was waiting at the airport with some of her crowd
I think they were a cult but I can't say that too loud, too loud

Pay me no mind , no, baby, no
Pay me no mind , no, baby, no

I've instructed my solicitor to punch you in the face
I'd do it myself but I'm in a state of grace
It's so hard to be vengeful when you're in this special place
I've instructed my solicitor to punch you in the face, in the face

Pay me no mind , no, baby, no
Pay me no mind , no, baby, no

I must integrate my feelings so I will be complete
Stop this splitting off that keeps me falling off my feet
Did I hear you say you think it's alright to lie?
Did I hear you say you think only fools toe the line? Toe the line?

Pay me no mind , no, baby, no
Pay me no mind , no, baby, no

NOW I LAY ME DOWN

Now I lay me down, with a sigh
And a soft smile of fond relief
Now I lay me down, for to die
Is the ending of mortal grief
Now I lay this ego down
While trumpet swans blow fanfares on the lake
For nobody's sake

Now I lay me down, just to be
Is the end all of what I seek
Now I lay me down, to be free
Of this hard ship I've sailed to see
Now I lay this ego down
While hungry crows drop chestnuts on the street
At my aching feet

Now I lay this ego down, put this mind to bed
Say good-bye to yesterday, while this sleepy head
Hears no one crying
Now I lay this ego down
While trumpet swans blow fanfares on the lake
For nobody's sake

ALMOST LIKE FATE

1998

I reached a fork in the road on my mail route back in the 1980's when I had all but decided to sell my Gibson J45 acoustic guitar and direct movies; like George Constanza deciding to become a color commentator for major league baseball. I looked down and spotted something gold in the dirt and bent down to pick it up. It was a rubber, Gibson J45 frig magnet, with the name 'Lyle' printed by hand in black ink on its face. I still have the magnet but sold the Gibson in 2009.

I LOST MY SENSE OF HUMOUR

I must say what must be said
My sense of humour is very nearly dead
It's really really hard to find
Ever since I heard about the Queen Of Hearts
I been soul searchin' but I must have lost
My way in the dark

I must say what must be said
My sense of humour used to be my daily bread
But now I'm hungry like a homeless man
They say that I must strengthen all that still remains
I been so steady but there's
Nothing that a body can claim

I lost my sense of humour but I don't know where
Maybe when I read that book by Baudelaire
Everytime I think about what Woody done
I get so upset I can't have no fun

I lost my sense of humour but I don't care
The way they act you'd think I was losin' my hair
Everybody's jokin' and they're feelin' alright
While I'm all alone, and that's not nice

I Should Be Commited

I should be committed
For being so committed
To somebody who
Treats me like you do
How many tears will it take
To get over you

I should be committed
For being so committed
To all the little things
You let me do
How many dreams will it take
To work this through

Please remember, baby,
Not to use the word 'crazy'
When you come and see me
In my rubber room
I'll try and hug you, momma,
If my arms will move

THE GURU'S LAMENT

Those who will be free put their faith in me
But like a wayward child refusing to be still
You wander everywhere in search of milk to spill

Please don't ask me why kindness makes you cry
You carry wounds so deep you mourn the gift of love
Foremost amongst my sheep I still have plenty of

Satellites, who orbit endlessly
I gotta like those who worship me
Out of sight, there's absolutely nothing to worry about
Unless you count your doubts

See them clear the way for my feet of clay
To be exalted is not all it's said to be
I must cope with those who wish they could be me

Please don't ask me why birds fall from the sky
You attach yourself to a dying thing
Close your eyes and wait and see what Santa brings

Saddle up and ride into the sun
Are you up for what must be done?
Farther up, beyond the lying mind
You're gonna see, what will be will be

I NEED ANOTHER KISS

I can't help it, I need another kiss
Reach up to my hungry mouth, give me what I miss
I'm begging to you, please, like a baby cries for milk
If you love me just a little, I will love you to the hilt

I can't help it, I need another kiss
Angels howl at midnight in the iridescent mist
Hooded doctors drive me to the barren edge of time
I can't help it and it ain't no crime

I can't help it, I need another kiss
How can you be leaving me hanging here like this
My tongue between my knees and my heart inside your purse
If I can't be going with you, I will go from bad to worse

I can't help it, I need another kiss
Angels howl at midnight in the iridescent mist
Hooded doctors drive me to the barren edge of time
I can't help it and it ain't no crime

Waiting here alone with my black-hearted phone
When it rings like a cold chain through my heart
It's the answer to my prayer, you say you'll meet me on the stair
And we'll climb where we can finish what we start

I can't help it, I need another kiss
Part your lips and take a trip into the abyss
There's just one thing that's worse than not having you at all
That's the moment when I've had you and my face is to the wall

BEING THE THINGS YOU DO

So many times, you've buttressed the mind
Against these thoughts, that seem so unkind
Giving them strength, they'll never really have
Fighting with a phantom self
That always seems to crash
Being the things you do

You may feel you can build a better you
Yet you'll depend on the things you think you do
There's no one acting here but life and life alone
No separate self making choices on its own
Being the things you do

What makes you think you're
Running around, all over town
Who told you that you move?
Who's really playing all of the parts
From finish to start
While you're silent through and through?

Bodies come and bodies sure do go
Nobody's body can interrupt the flow
You've been watching your own body pass the time
When it goes you'll know
You're not the me and mine
Being the things you do

Death is really nothing of the kind
Just an end to the memories that bind
Love in light, flowing free without a doubt
Lets you know your life is really not about
Being the things you do

What makes you think you're
Running around, all over town
Who told you that you move?
Who's really playing all of the parts
From finish to start
While you're silent through and through

Psychic friends and the cold, blue hand of time
Know your fate's identical to mine
Step aside and see there's nothing to protect
Dot your t's and cross your I's while you reject
Being the things you do

ON THE TRAIL OF BROKEN HEARTS

On the trail of broken hearts
Each one split by Cupid's dart
I track the woman perfect as a rose
She has sown the seeds of shame
In the men who've fanned her flame
Then blown away like smoke upon the breeze

I'm the Wiesenthal of Texas
On the trail of broken hearts
I know she's waiting for me
Somewhere in these parts
We are star-crossed like the planets
And when we two collide
On the trail of broken hearts
I will have her for my bride

On the trail of broken hearts
I collect my bloodhounds barks
And feed them to computers, I don't care
I will steal the crutch of faith
From the crippled human race
And follow her forever everywhere

I'm the Wiesenthal of Texas
On the trail of broken hearts
I know she's waiting for me
Somewhere in these parts
We are star-crossed like the planets
And when we two collide
On the trail of broken hearts
I will have her for my bride

On the trail of broken hearts
I can see our wedding march
My blushing bride in black all over me
We will celebrate the day
In our own peculiar way
With shoes and rice and holes
Where hearts should be

I'm the Wiesenthal of Texas
On the trail of broken hearts
I know she's waiting for me
Somewhere in these parts
We are star-crossed like the planets
And when we two collide
On the trail of broken hearts
I will have her for my bride

WHERE YOU GOIN', DARLIN' DAUGHTER

Where you goin', darlin' daughter, didn't your Daddy raise
   you right?
Isn't it true you're smoking pot or maybe I just ain't seein' right
Where you goin,' little one, why do you torture me?
What's that punk got up his sleeve to make you wanna leave?

Tell me where you goin', darlin', must it be away from me?
Tell me where you goin,' little one, I'm too blind to see

Where you goin', darlin' daughter, doesn't your Mother's
   feelings count?
It wouldn't have hurt more if you'd shot her
You really know how to let her down
Where you goin,' little one, why do you torture me?
What's that punk got up his sleeve to make you wanna leave?

Tell me where you goin', darlin', must it be away from me?
Tell me where you goin,' little one, I'm too blind to see

Where's she goin' our darlin' daughter?
She don't know her left hand from her right
Everything we have taught her she treats like so much bad advice
Where you goin,' little one, so far away from home?
I will never forgive you for leaving us alone

Tell me where you goin', darlin', must it be away from me?
Tell me where you goin,' little one, I'm too blind to see

BEAUTY LOOKS AWAY

Beauty Looks Away

John Lyle

1995

I have had two experiences in my life that transcend everything I have known. The first was in 1969 and was an understanding that what is permanent and real is subjective and sublime and untouchable in its majesty and grace. It is also my self. The second experience was in 1971, and was a glimpse of the wonderfully mysterious but simple power that takes care of every event I appear to infuse with pride, shame or indifference. This is also an aspect of my self. The only thing I could say at that time was, 'there is absolutely nothing to worry about'. Within days of this last experience, 'I' had forgotten both events and become embroiled in the life I describe in my songs. That way of life was to last until I hit a wall of despair in 1986 and remembered what I know to be true, which is knowing itself. From then on, there has not been a day when I have not remembered who I am. The losses we all endure as a price for having loved became for me, although sometimes excruciatingly painful, natural in the light of understanding the temporal nature of this sporting life. The relentless, primal message I hear in the songs that have come through me is that I do not exist as an individual entity and that my so-called achievements and failures belong to life itself and are short-lived appearances. What is behind and supports life is infinitely and eternally beautiful and is my true being. What always is and will always be is what I really am.

SOMEONE'S CALLING

Someone's calling through the wind and the rain
Someone's calling out again and again

Who am I
Who am I

Someone's calling, I can hear the refrain

Beat the drum slowly, we are mourning a friend
Beat the drum slowly and then beat it again

Someone's calling, see the root of the tree
Someone's calling, you have always been free

Who am I
Who am I

Someone's calling, I can hear the refrain

Beat the drum slowly, we are mourning a friend
Beat the drum slowly and then beat it again

Someone's calling, come away from this land
Someone's calling, be as quick as you can

STRAIGHT ON DOWN THE LINE

A sentimental wishing well where the bubbles never stop
However many feet I fall, I feel I'm at the top
You're in the groove, straight on down straight on down the line

Standing at the pony rail with puddles in your hands
Dreaming of the monkey faces you can't understand
You're in the groove, straight on down straight on down the line

Guess you better wait a while til the glue begins to set
Honey, what a joke it is to be caught outside the net
You're in the groove, straight on down straight on down the line

Many times I see your name but it falls beneath my teeth
I know I gotta go again and paint my hidden grief
You're in the groove, straight on down straight on down the line

Still you cannot feel your fists beating at the rain
Jumping in the humble few who chew their tongues again
You're in the groove, straight on down straight on down the line

Maybe now the crystal falls deep inside the track
Shatter all the needle balls you treasured for a map
You're in the groove, straight on down straight on down the line

Pretty Penny found today a voice beside the wood
Stolen dreams to mark the day you did but what you could
You're in the groove, straight on down straight on down the line

Sleepin' in the bed beside the one who knows me too
Laughing in his letters for the wave was not to you
You're in the groove, straight on down straight on down the line

The shepherd's heart is broken now, he's drowning in his fears
The matron saint of duty has confounded him with tears
You better get it together, get it together, get it together
You better get it together, get it together

COUNTRY HARVEST TIME

When the apple is ripe it will fall
There's nothin' will stop it at all
Who's afraid of yesterday
At Country Harvest Time

Silent Light's sightless sight
Sees no one inside
Monkey talk's in the dock
At Country Harvest Time

When the wind blows your name from my lips
And my finger finds no need to grip
Now and here all doubts are cleared
At Country Harvest Time

Silent Light's sightless sight
Sees no one inside
Monkey talk's in the dock
At Country Harvest Time

You think you've the ghost of a chance
To change the steps of the dance
Armageddon with a smile
At Country Harvest Time

ALL THAT BINDS

The mind is deep and quiet
Seeing all that binds
But it's just a pale reflection
Of what I cannot find

All these thoughts and feelings
Happen over there
On the battleground of sight and sound
Where nothing's ever fair

Living in the moment
Seeing all that binds
Leaving all the torment
Many moons behind
Really wanting nothing
Letting go what comes
Abandoning this hunted thing
That's always on the run

♪ HUMORS

1985

I was a big American songbook fan before they called it that. Porter, Berlin, Kern and Gershwin were my gods because melody rules for me. I've been told more than once by the people who know that I have a gift for melody and if I could only hook up with a good lyricist they might be able to do something for me

HOW ROMANTIC OF ME

All locked into something the psychics can't control
And the rainbow-fingered hordes are in a hole
With all of their possessions, beyond grief and past the dawn
While I work to hold back my yellow yawn

How romantic of me, how romantic of me
How romantic of me all along

How romantic of me to have eaten my degree
And passed it, Lord, I must learn how to ski
How romantic of me to keep my interest in a sack
And how romantic to keep keeping track

How romantic of me, how romantic of me
How romantic of me, coming back

All along the river inspectors take their counts
While up the country gurus climb the mount
Holy little brothers bathe their souls in burning bleach
While I work on my music on the beach

How romantic of me, how romantic of me
How romantic of me not to preach

BLASTED IN HOPE

In and out and out and in
The ocean breezes blow
I been waiting for that sweet ride
Like an ordinary orphan in the sand
Let me take my stand, soul dance in your hand
To tinsel tunes from silver stars, oh baby

Sweet low down and all around
The lone star whistle blows
I been trying to make connection
With my fast and lonesome Southern Dixie Flyer
Stream-lined and winding fire
Stone-blown through the sky
To what's behind our lost tomorrow, baby

Eat the flesh and suck the bone
And drink my blood like wine
I'll come crashing through your window
Like a hot and heartless steaming Philistine
Full out to break your spine,
Smash your dreams on the door
To what's behind our lost tomorrow, baby

Longing eyes are hypnotized
Inside the last sunbow
Let's protect the same illusion
While the harvest moon is still a memory,
Eventual ecstasy's a blockade to the star
And what's behind our lost tomorrow, baby

OH, MY WIND

Oh the wind is like a friend of mine, she is fickle to a fault
One minute solid as a tree, and the next not worth her salt

That's why she's so fine, that's way she's not mine
Think of all she's touched, still she gives so much...
Oh, my wind, where you been, I thought you said you'd write
Oh, my wind, where you been, I waited up all night

Oh the wind is like a friend of mine, she has a temper like
   a carving knife
She doesn't do it to be mean, but now and then she'll take a slice

That's why she's so fine, that's why she's not mine
Think of all she's touched, still she gives so much...
Oh, my wind, where you been I thought you said you'd write
Oh, my wind, where you been, I waited up all night

Some blue Monday I'll be under such a heavy cloud
With no way to turn my lonely head but down
Then my wind will blow on in and turn my life around
She'll come runnin', I'll bet she's thumbin', just outside of town

Oh the wind is like a friend of mine, her fatal flaw is her
   saving grace
If she didn't get around, I'd never see her lovely face

That's why she's so fine, that's why she's not mine
Think of all she's touched, still she gives so much...
Oh, my wind, where you been, I thought you said you'd write
Oh, my wind, where you been, I waited up all night

♪ I SAW GOD

By accident I took a double dose of L.S.D.
I saw God inside my mirror and He looked a lot like me
Maybe two, three inches shorter, and a little sparse on top
He was cleaning his glasses, He was cleaning his glasses
With the blood of a lamb chop

I said, God, what you doin' hung out in my mirror
He said takin' a vacation, man, you never see me here
I said, God, I see you now, and when I wanna shave
I'll have to drop my razor, I'll have to drop my razor.
I'll have to drop my razor and wave

God said, what have you been eating
I said Owsley's L.S.D.
He said, go and count your marbles, kid
You're lucky you still see
They're not here, they're over there, He said
So over there I go, and count my marbles
Count my marbles, count my marbles slow

When wonder piled on wonder up my alley I can see
God inside a cat's-eye cleaning salmon with a key

WE MUST KNOW

We must know what really happened (gonna tell ya)
We must know what really happened (I can smell ya)

Mr. Hollywood came knockin' at the door
He said, what's a big star like you doin', baby
Not working anymore
Big star said, I don't know, maybe it's my age
Sometimes I think they're laughing at me
Then he flew into a rage

We must know what really happened (gonna tell ya)
We must know what really happened (I can smell ya)

Big star spelled his drink and swore into the Montecito sun
Mr. Hollywood said, baby, wait'll you hear what I done
We're on the red-eye to the apple, we'll get a limo to Times Square
We'll find a most outstanding mugging, the paparazzi will be there
You'll save someone or other from the vicious junkie hordes
And when the story hits the tabloids it will strike responsive chords

We must know what really happened (gonna tell ya)
We must know what really happened (I can smell ya)

Now wait a little minute, said the big star as he hid
His face behind his glass, he said let's not and say we did
And that's what really happened, and that's why he's back to work
And I'll bet you thought the big star wasn't nothin',
Wasn't nothin', wasn't nothin', wasn't nothin' but a jerk!

WHEN I'M A P. H. D.

When I'm a P.H.D., no one will dare to question me
Except the other P.H.D.'s, but not when I'm on TV
Where everyone will worship me, oh Jehovah!

P.H.D., P.H.D., I will be a P.H.D
With a bona fide degree made out to me

When I'm a P.H.D., I'm gonna share my salary
With all my family for everything they did for me
To help me finally get to be

A P.H.D., P.H.D., I will be a P.H.D
With a bona fide degree made out to me

At our parties all us smarties will let down our hair
Stand on a chair, bare as you dare, you can stare
But we won't care

When I'm a P.H.D., no ivory tower will fall on me
In my professional building by the sea
Where I'll teach everyone to be
A successful P.H.D like me, why don't you be like me

GOING THROUGH THE MOTIONS

This little bubble, this black cauldron of trouble
The starry-eyed call Mother Earth
Can blow all to hell, clean the air of the smell
But that'll just add to my mirth

Going through the moves, going through the motions
Everything we choose is a preconceived notion
There are no heroes and there are no villains
Just us little computer children

Going through the moves, going through the motions
Every means is an end, every end is a potion

Going through the moves, going through the motions
Every means is an end, every end is a potion
Fight fire with water, fight hate with love
Wake up before push comes to shove

No one deserves credit, no one deserves blame
No one deserves a fortune, no one deserves fame
No one deserves a great big mansion or a ghetto full of pain
No one deserves what they get, but they get it just the same

Going through the moves, going through the motions
A new world awaits based on the notion
We accept one another like the wind and the rain
Free as the birds and bees in our chains

RANCHERO

We have ranchero, we have mucho dinero,
In our world not a care-o,
Ay yi yi yi yi yi

We can depend on our hacienda
To defend us when the four winds blow
No matter how bad the weather may be,
We always will have somewhere to go

So when the clouds frown upon us
And the rains try to drown us
And the wind is beating at our door
There's a song we'll be making
While the snowflakes are flaking
And it goes like this, Senor

We have ranchero, we have mucho dinero,
In our world not a care-o,
Ay yi yi yi yi yi

♪ HARD COVER VIRGINS

1978

John Murray owns points on many of my songs for having en-
hanced them with the beauty of his playing for over forty years.
Two songs John and I wrote together and which appear on
Hard-Cover Virgins epitomize his gifts for both melody writing
and guitar playing. He also supplied the images which formed
the basis for the lyrics for both these songs *Life is a Breeze* and
Close Your Eyes.

BLOOD RIVER

My ancestors were amphibian
They crawled out of the Caribbean
Tooth and fin they fought
To make good their escape
But like the rain that brings us rivers
And the blood cleaned by my liver
There ain't nothin' gonna get away from fate

We're AWOL, that's all
Even a wonder like Niagara falls
When Neptune cups the conch
I'll be piped aboard a launch
And buried in the middle of the sea

Blood river, gougin' out a gorge
Blood river, floodin' Valley Forge
Blood river, pulsin' up a storm inside my wrist

It tumbles towards the ocean
Just as if it had some notion
Of a promise made to keep a sacred tryst
It shows this Land o' Goshen
Cyclic poetry in motion
And it teaches godless children to exist

We can't build too near the current
'cause there is no real deterrent
To the savage grace of water gone bizarre
We can heap sandbags forever
Drown the Lord in our endeavour
But we might as well try harnessing a star

LIFE IS A BREEZE

Life is a breeze when we're down by the sea
We are mellow, baby, just you and I
Easy to please, makes no difference what season
We are happy to be really alive

Racing along the golden shore
We will stop and stare into the sun
When day is done
Life is a breeze when we're down by the sea
Life is a breeze for you and me

Combing the beach we are way out of reach
Of tomorrow, we live just for today
Breathing the air, we can feel all our cares
And our sorrow sinking deep in the bay

Racing along the golden shore
We will stop and stare into the sun
When day is done
Life is a breeze when we're down by the sea
Life is a breeze for you and me

Now the moon is on the scene
Like a spell, she casts her beam over dark waves
We are lost inside a dream
There's no place where we would rather be but here

We have a home where the sand, wind and foam
Make us mellow, baby, just you and I
Easy to please, makes no difference what season
We are happy to be really alive

Racing along the golden shore
We will stop and stare into the sun
When day is done
Life is a breeze when we're down by the sea
Life is a breeze for you and me

Lyrics for this song co-written with John Murray

BLUE PICTURES IN THE TUNNEL

7:30 and another dirty show to go and see
It's insane to be trusting, the minussing or plussing
Of a movie God has meant to be
To a filth-catching fraction, of a filth-catching faction
Whose coming attraction is dissatisfaction with me
Blue pictures in the tunnel and I still can't close my eyes

Oh, the love scenes were daring, they crossed into hate
And the requisite swearing was really ornate
Torture and killing are more than just chilling
When meant to reflect the innate

Bring my scissors and blue pencil, honey, let me get it done
I'll take sex out of violence and sound out of silence
And watch folks require their refunds
Like those cold, cheated creatures in those old, second features
Crawling for cover and howling for colour from me
Blue pictures in the tunnel and I still can't close my eyes

Oh, the love scenes were daring, they crossed into hate
And the requisite swearing was really ornate
Torture and killing are more than just chilling
When meant to reflect the innate

Da da da da da da da, they got me nailed to the marquee
I'm pure box office boff; ain't they never gonna switch
    that power off
They come from everywhere to see me bleed
They're a foregone conclusion; I'm their nude, transfused illusion
Passin' out the popcorn, and prayin', for God's sake, for
    some God's speed
Blue pictures in the tunnel and I still can't close my eyes

MY ADDLED ESSENCE

Let's stop our foolin' around
And let's make a pact to keep
Our heads on the ground
'cause daddy started worryin'
The night he found us swallowin'
Stones on an empty stretch
Of our imaginations

His love for us will just die
If we continue low down living
High on the sly
He caught me creepin' out of dreams
And into schemes to honour themes
He's built his old life around
Solidifying his station

Break down our network of lies,
And bury our hypocrisy deep in our eyes
And hope the smoky signals
Of deception never come in between
What we're thinking
And what we are doing for daddy

Daddy-o, you know we're doin'
What we're doin' for you, for you
And if that's the kind of lovin'
That our poppa's got a-comin'
Well, you know he better love us too

3, 4, 5 to one as reckless as I
A daddy is a matchstick and a limit's the sky

111

Larkin' is my business, I'd be livin' a lie
So, so long crooked straight life
I'm leavin', you ain't life, behind

WATER WORKS

What a thrill to climb over the hill
And find you takin' a leak
I can't help but pant when I happen to chance
On what it is I do seek
Water works, I see your water works

I got a hench that my monkey wrench
Is what is needed here
I bet by heck , when I plumb your depths
You'll be bound to shed a tear
Water works, I see your water works

Ain't it rare how a pipe can bear
The necessary juices of life
With a brace at the base and a smile on my face
I'm ready to make you my wife
As long as your good conduit matches mine
We will never ever need to be primed
And soon the pitter pat of little drips
Will mean the start of our own water line

I feel the sap risin' in my tap, oh my hose is almost froze
If you don't let me into your big sink
I'll be petrified in this pose
Water works, I need your water works
Like a child of Jesus needs his knees
I need your water works

MY COLD IS GONE

If any one had said, hey, get to bed and beat your cold
I'd have burned my clothes and paid the sky to rain
When it comes to getting well, my friends can go to hell
Can't they see I'm a self-healed man, and

My cold is gone, not that last one but that one that really
     lingered on
I fought it like the fading moon combats the dawn
I hung around like a fingernail

Sometimes now, I wake up in the morning with an anvil
     in my head
And a blacksmith beating on it with a red hot piece of lead
And my throat so sore I'd like a war so I could be dead
Then I remember what I said

My cold is gone, not that last one but that one that really
     lingered on
I fought it like the fading moon combats the dawn
I hung around like a fingernail

NATIVE SON OF THE FIRST CAUSE

It's clear to me that countries are in business to survive
That the measure of a nation is its patriotic pride
But boundaries breed bigotry and bigotry's a lie
Unless of course it all depends on where you draw the line

Native son of the First Cause, naked son of the First Cause
Like Robinson Caruso I'm an island in the sky
And I'm gonna build a parapet so I'll be fortified

Universal brotherhood is more than just a dream
Cain brained Abel and the Germans ate the Jews
Brothers bloodied up the stream
We are all in the same lifeboat, though we've blown it full of holes
Sink or swim, we're next of kin, but who's to have control?

Native son of the First Cause, naked son of the First Cause
Like Robinson Caruso I'm an island in the sky
And I'm gonna build a parapet so I'll be fortified

There's a little bit of Hitler in the saintliest of men
So I'd just as soon a saint appeared, but saints don't ever win
So I'll settle for some bureau cats whose skins aren't made of flag
To meld the helms and overwhelm these selfish scallywags

Native son of the First Cause, naked son of the First Cause
Like Robinson Caruso I'm an island in the sky
And I'm gonna build a parapet so I'll be fortified

WONDERIN'

Darlin', I been wonderin' about you
Do you do the things you used to do
Like brushin' down your daddy's mare
Baking cakes for county fairs
Wish you could be wonderin' 'bout me too

Yeah, you got me wonderin'
If our love is at its end
Won't you take my hand again
And stop my wonderin'

Darlin' I been wonderin' about when
We were on our wasted honeymoon
You wanted love and I got lost
Now I just can't pay the cost
What's this lonesome cowpoke gonna do

Yeah, you got me wonderin'
If our love is at its end
Won't you take my hand again
And stop my wonderin'

I may be a failure, but, honey, I must tell ya
There is more to me than what I didn't do
You're alone out on the ranch
Now give this buckaroo a chance
To prove what didn't happen isn't true

Yeah, you got me wonderin'
If our love is at its end
Won't you take my hand again
And stop my wonderin'

GUNFIGHT AT THE OCCULT CORRAL

Dead man on a new horizon, colder than polarity
He still defies my dream
That I'm night watchman for the sacred passion
That's descending like a dinner date I'm terrified to keep

Here's a toast to the man in the ground
Let's have another round for the man in the ground
Seven came eleven and the odds cut him down
Like a flash in the plan he's gone

What makes God's children wanna die
To prove they've been crucified
Is life only lonely lies? Is hope the same as charity
And faith the only hope for me? What a tragic carpet ride!

Here's a toast to the man in the ground
Let's have another round for the man in the ground
Seven came eleven and the odds cut him down
Like a flash in the plan he's gone

Living on a ledge of sadness, like a man without a secret
He was just too damned alone. Living on the edge of madness,
Til the show was closed-short-circuit
'cause a tape looped around his soul

Here's a toast to the man in the ground
Let's have another round for the man in the ground
Seven came eleven and the odds cut him down
Like a flash in the plan he's gone

If his scales were just, dead even, they were tipped towards
    the devil
Death was all that he could do, but if our hearts can fill with evil,
We can also build an Eden, and there's one thing I can do

Propose a toast to the man in the ground
Let's have another round for the man in the ground
Seven came eleven and the odds cut him down
Like a flash in the plan he's gone

For Graeme Smith

THE PLOT WIDENS

I can see a day when this old earth will be a mess of tombs
Can't you people understand this world is running out of room

So if you gotta die, be a real good guy
Go and find another spot to rot
Away you go, so long, good-bye

Be real great, evaporate, or will your bod to the sea
Be nice, and sacrifice your ashes to the breeze

Things are lookin' bad when even graveyards get a ton of mail
To whom is it addressed? Some lucky stiff'll get it without fail

So if you gotta die, be a real good guy
Go and find another spot to rot
Away you go, so long, good-bye

Everybody's mother must finally be laid to rest
Put her in a place where she can still do what she does do best
Make meals taste like wow! This manure ain't from no
     Guernsey cow
Go and throw her on the compost heap
She'll help to make some tasty chow

So if you gotta die, be a real good guy
Go and find another spot to rot
Away you go, so long, good-bye

THE WOO WOO INTO TOWN

Things are getting' boring 'cause my wife just caught me snoring
Now she says I got to paint the garage
I'd do it in a minute but there ain't no money in it
And I don't work for nothin' but cash
Little Jimmy broke the cat; Lord, I'm leavin,' where's my hat?
This duplex daddy's way past due for a blast

I take the woo woo into town, and then I really get around
I go to parties where there ain't any floor
And when it's time to leave, I got a hunch you won't believe
I can't, 'cause there ain't any door
I take the woo woo into town, and then I really get around
And then I got to take the boo hoo back

My better half is waitin' when I get in kinda late 'n' then
She asks me where I got the giraffe
I tell her it's a mystery, just a hunk of recent history
And I'll use it when I paint the garage
Little Jimmy calls the cops; Lord, I hit him with the mop
This duplex daddy's way past due for a blast

I take the woo woo into town, and then I really get around
I go to parties where there ain't any floor
And when it's time to leave, I got a hunch you won't believe
I can't, 'cause there ain't any door
I take the woo woo into town, and then I really get around
And then I got to take the boo hoo back

They got the place surrounded and I'm feelin' mighty hounded
When I get back on the boo hoo on time
I tell 'em this misunderstanding is a product of mishandling

By my son and that there woman of mine
The cops begin to go, little Jimmy hollars, no!
Stay and watch my daddy paint the giraffe

I take the woo woo into town and then I really get around
I go to parties where there ain't any floor
And when it's time to leave, I got a hunch you won't believe
I can't, 'cause there ain't any door
I take the woo woo into town, and then I really get around
And then I got to take the boo hoo back

DON'T STRING UP THE THROWBACK

The caveman was a rapist, no he wasn't very fair
He'd hit a woman on the head, and drag her by the hair
To his bed of bones, and while she'd moan, he'd have his
    filthy way
And if she cooked when he'd partook, he'd guess he'd let her stay

It's strange how times have changed, and people with them too
Now a man can crawl and pawn his balls and still not get a screw
So it's a little short of shocking that that guy might change
    his plan
And lay in wait to rape his date like Joe Orangutan

Chorus:
Don't string up the throwback, turn him loose in Ontario
On the throwback's reservation, where the throwbacks all can go
And sew their wild potatoes, and see their sucklings grow
And if they act like animals, at least we won't have to know

They say it's not that simple; I say don't be so hard
How can a man be better, after living under guard
It's time for a new 'down under,' even if it's up on Mars
I'd rather live in a spaceship than die behind bars

CLOSE YOUR EYES

Baby, rest beneath this tree
Beside your lady
Feel her fingertips upon your brow
Tired minds are unwinding now
Here within her arms
It's warm and shady
You can feel the leaves
Caress the boughs
You're adrift on a tender cloud

Close your eyes, the bluebirds fly
Wind and trees compose a melody
Close your eyes, the bluebirds fly
Across the sea of time

Baby, rest beneath this tree
Beside your lady
Whispers in the meadow say the stream
Leads the way to an endless dream

Close your eyes, the bluebirds fly
Wind and trees compose a melody
Close your eyes, the bluebirds fly
Across the sea of time

Lyrics for this song co-written with John Murray

BOOTLEG POWERHEAD

1971

Leonard Cohen's and my paths crossed when I met the movie director Robert Altman's daughter Christine Johnson. She loved my songs and introduced me to her father who was shooting *Mcabe And Mrs. Miller* in Vancouver. He had decided he wanted to build the movie around Cohen's album, but was having trouble getting the rights. So Christine asked me to write a song for the movie. She gave me the script and I wrote *The Showdown Might Be Tragedy*, which appeared on my first album *Bootleg Powerhead*. Altman had me record all the songs from Cohen's album to use as a backup in case Cohen wouldn't agree to allow his album to be used in the movie, which of course he did. Then they all left town.

RIVERS OF STONE

Neon Bride, please come inside, you've sanctified the street
Now kiss my doors and bless the boards that run beneath my feet

Neon Bride, please look alive and leave these streams of stone
And search my banks and breathe your soul into my telephones

Can't you hear the silver sirens scream at sickle moons?
Electric tyrants make my life a room and a road that leads
    nowhere

Neon Bride, forget your pride and pave the paths to hell
The street of lies runs through your eyes
And the darkness knows you well

Neon Bride, you're not alive, your veins are coursed with gas
Your life is light and like as not your light might never last

Can't you feel the fires burning all along the dream
Glass hearts yearning by a silver stream
Laid of stones that roll nowhere

LIVING THROUGH THE BLUES

Missed a lot of lovin' down in Tennessee
It takes a lot of lovin' for a fool like me
Livin' through the blues I'm like a fricasseed chickadee

Smoked a lot of dope and I'm an aeroplane
Suppose I'm never gonna see things quite the same again
Livin' through the blues I'm like a fricasseed chickadee

See the little lady, boys, she sets my soul on fire
I'm the kind of shady toy should be her pacifier

If I run out of atoms on the Santa Fe
Think I'll pretend I'm Jimmie Rogers in a Chevrolet
Livin' through the blues I'm like a fricasseed chickadee

Had eternal contacts 'til they disappeared
Guess they're somewhere in the middle of the hemisphere
Livin' through the blues I'm like a fricasseed chickadee

It blows my mind to find that I'm still on parole
I'm dreaming on the outskirts of my only soul
Livin through the blues I'm like a fricasseed chickadee

KATHERINE ROSS'S HOSSES

I wish that I was one of Katherine Ross's hosses
We'd ride the range to the silver strains of me
She'd ride astride and I'd feel obliged to wander
Wherever she might want the range to be
Can't you see me now? I ain't no plow horse
I'm a saucy, tossy Ross horse
With my mistress mounting me so wild and free
And if my libido's showin', bet your spurs I'll be growin'
Palomino, pal of mine, you're gonna do me proud

I wish that I was one of Katherine Ross's hosses
From Tinsel Town to the sylvan mound we'd roam
We'd stake our claim and she'd call my name- 'Flame Wonder,'
My five-card pard, you're never gonna let me down
Can't you see us now, ain't we a picture
Worth a thousand story-book words?
Saddle pals with saddle bags of saddle songs
'cause that long, long trail gets dusty and it helps
To have a trusty saddle tune or two to fun the miles away

I wish that I was one of Katherine Ross's hosses
No hitchin' posts'd come between her steed and her
We wouldn't ford love's stream, we'd ride her sparkling clean
True waters into the setting sun for ever more
Can't you see us now, aint we a western, fairy-tale dream
We're the best one to slip out of here in such a lonesome time
And if horses could get married to a starlet, not to a carriage
We'd no longer wander shamelessly in sin

LIES ARE ONLY LETTERS

Reverberating into the innermost reaches of his private brain
Hal Humble tests the sad, sad state of his joke; fully realizing
Lies are only letters to your heartsick mother's
Lonesome baby child, oh no, oh no, oh no, oh no!

Complicating matters in the strangest way but with a sense of flow
Hal's Hannah smiles a quick 'Hello! I know you know I know.'
Fully realizing lies are only letters to your heartsick lover's
Lonesome baby smile, oh no, oh no, oh no, oh no!

Calibrating constancies across the room and through the
    great divide
Hal Humble hears his Hannah sigh, 'I guess I'm still alone.'
Fully realizing lies are only letters from your heartsick lover's
Mother's broken child, oh no, oh no, oh no, oh no!

Mitigating circumstances with his hands and with his sounds
    of love
Hal Humble makes his special love across his Hannah's eyes;
Fully realizing lies and ties and alibis intensify
Your lullaby of love- oh no, oh no, oh no, oh no!

KEEP THE BANNERS FLYING

My heart's been sent to heaven
And the same old used to be
Still lingers on beside the riverside
That holds a line on me
Holds a line on me

The dream is an illusion
And it never comes again
Until the ocean tries to take you back
To where you've always been
Where you've always been

And when the cave on sugar mountain
Is the only home I count on, I'm a fool
And when the grave beneath Death Valley
Is my mind inside an alley, I'll be cool

A series of explosions
From the leftest field there is
Has come and left me with a big desire
To break into the biz, break into the biz

The scenes are always changing
And I haven't found the key
But when I sing this song the ghost of God
Comes sailing home to me, sailing home to me

And when the cave on sugar mountain
Is the only home I count on, I'm a fool
And when the grave beneath Death Valley
Is my mind inside an alley, I'll be cool

HELLO BUDDY

Well, I know your lazy susans, and I know your easy chairs
And I know your swinging hammocks sleepy-two time
    your despair
And I know the hours you kill spending seconds splitting hairs
Cannot keep you from your purpose, cannot keep you from
    the stair
And I wish that I could organize my mind

Well, I know that your polemics, comprehensive and bizarre
Could get me on your band-wagon if I was a movie star
But I'm having trouble shaking, I no longer have a car
And my best friend's wife has left me in this lonesome,
    homely bar
And I wish I had a dollar for a dime

'cause I'm still a little thirsty and there's still a lot of time
'cause those big, old hands keep slowin' and stopping on my dime
And the world owes me a drink and I just want what is mine
And I'll hate the man who says you're not my friend

Well I think my stool is screwing me up into my hair
And is that our old bar-tender with his arm up in the air?
And is that a knife he's holding? Well it's just not hardly fair
After all the time I've spent here and with all I've had to bear
Do you think you have somewhere that you can spare?

DEATHLESS SONG

If the sun don't burn the tears away from all our ragged dreams
I'll be the one to try to prove that I am more than what I seem
If the steel, insane insistent rain from my old, lost guitar
Can be a groove for me and a tune for you, help me raise the bar

Love's a wicked word when you're a crazy cagey fool
Beneath the silver wires and diamond knives in time
Left alone and stoned into the heart of Emmot's Zone
I know that everything that's passed ain't left behind

And so I'll meet you in the countryside a love affair from now
You know, I pray the breeze that feeds the trees
Will hold us there somehow

New bluebirds and old blue-devils war inside of me
I guess a deathless song's the only way I have to set you free

Feel the blue cool burn of frontier justice in the yearning
That we're yearning every time we want to cry
I'm the part of you that wants to be the part of me
That wants to come into the sky while I'm alive

If the sun don't burn the tears away from all our ragged dreams
I'll be the one to try to prove that I am more than what I seem

THE SHOWDOWN MIGHT BE TRAGEDY

When our trust is in the gambler and the odds are on the wall
And all the whores can beg for rain-checks
While their johns lose all recall
And when our minds are always busy mailing letters to the sea
It's the show-off age and it's the show-off stage
And the showdown might be tragedy

When the preacher is a shadow hidden deep within himself
And when the church is just a house around a promise to protect
And when our eyes are always searching for an empty ecstasy
It's the show-off age and it's the show-off stage
And the showdown might be tragedy

When the sun can break a window and a word can break
    my heart
Into a bleeding, screaming billion scandalizing counterparts
And when the dawn buys benediction and your voice is clemency
It's the show-off age and it's the show-off stage
And the showdown might be tragedy

When the showdown is a shoot-out and the stakes are after all
Just a price to pay for praying for another bang-up brawl
And when our masks are disappearing into naked comedy
It's the show-off age and it's the show-off stage
And the showdown might be tragedy

LOSE

I can't read between the lines between the lines
I can't say the words that touch off a good time
only stop myself from having a good try
at the fly ball that is lost up in the sky
the limit's known to me alone all by myself in emmot's zone
you can rock the night away and say your prayers
you can throw the key away and say you care
about the wheres and hows and whys you're not there
and why you don't believe that it's not fair
for me to care about you, for me to share what I lose
think I'll close my eyes and dream another song
after all I've memorized it won't be long
before some new someone else happens along
and I get a chance to prove I'm always wrong
for you and your friends, tell me the truth, don't I lose?
I can't see between the brackets of taipan
but I have a very special friend who can
she looks in on jack the ripper in between
and paints self-portraits of the many things she's seen
like something dark, and noah's ark
that block the stream, confuse her dream
she can't see as far as she has never seen
she can't be as far as she has never been
but she sure as hell can push you off the boat
yes and seal her plastic hands around your throat
she brings ice-box blues and sad good news
worn out toys for broken boys
used to be that we all slept around her bed
with the dreams of her dead lovers for our head

of the crowd that melted rosebuds on the sleigh
and washed the guts of fallen angels down the drain
we have had enough, she played too rough
we've lost the pooh, now we're all through

Lyrics for this song co-written with Garry MacPherson

LOST IN THE DREAM

The day of grace was up today, I'm shipwrecked in your arms
All my false alarms ring true, old buddy, I'm blue
Derek's bass can fill the space between our tear-stained eyes
Above the seizing lies we knew, oh, old buddy, I knew

And you know, I love to play the fool,
Capsized and baptized and scared to be in school
But if you're gonna leave me, you better leave me paralyzed
'cause I'm telling you now, I'm in love with your eyes
I think it's the truth, I'm in love with your eyes

Love to be the shooting star to suck you to the screen
Just like Eddie Dean come true, oh, old buddy, come true
I can sing a wave length out beyond the no mile reef
Because of my belief in you, oh old buddy, in you

Undertow, drag me to the deep
Wrap your arms around me and rock my brain to sleep
But I don't guess a coma's gonna keep me crystallized
'cause I'm telling you now, I m in love with their eyes
I think it's the truth, I'm in love with your eyes

It's hard as nails to try to find a silver thing to say
When you're a shipwrecked castaway
Like me, oh, old buddy like me

SINGLES

When my son Pax was born in 1978 I wanted to give him a song he could carry through his life. John Murray and I were writing together at the time, and he had a beautiful melody I thought would suit the spirit of what I wanted to do. Although John's emphasis was on writing commercially, he generously allowed me to use his melody for our song 'Pax'. All these years later, I would not change a word of what I had to say to my wonderful son.

You Broke Right Down and Cried

You were nameless
In the loss of your grief
You thought that old time feeling
Was beyond your reach, *and then*
You broke right down and cried

You built an altar
As high as you could
You cut an old growth forest
For the firewood *and then*
You broke right down and cried

You were stranded there
With nothing more to say
Why did you even start
What had to end that way

You fought a battle
You knew you would lose
Against a host of shadows
And a world of blues *and then*
You broke right down and cried

You climbed a mountain
Like your heart didn't care
You held your arms wide open
To the cold night air *and then*
You broke right down and cried

Before the falling sun
Deserts the hollow ground
They'll all come runnin'
To hear you scream out loud

You remembered
You always exist
Behind a world of sorrow
In a sea of bliss, *and then*
You broke right down and cried

A Break in the Weather

You felt you had to post
A big storm warning
When I said sail with me
It was as if you'd sabotaged
My moorings
Leaving me all at sea

Now there's a break in the weather
And I know that's a break for me
Now and forever, a break in the weather
Is all it's cracked up to be

Cumulonimbus, nimbostratus, uh huh,
Both fail to appear
All the clouds got wrinkled brows
'cause they aren't wanted here

If I was some old weatherman
From Florida
Tell you what I'd do
Find me a hurricane
That's made to order
And I'd name it after you

But now there's a break in the weather
And I know that's a break for me
Now and forever, a break in the weather
Is all it's cracked up to be

KNOW THE RIVER

You're the captain of your craft
And you must know it fore and aft
If you're to get to put into
Your port of call

But that won't be enough for
When the river's ways get rough
And you're caught out in
The middle of a squall

Then you must know the river
Know how to give her
The respect she will more than demand
Know the river when your timbers shiver
And you long to be back on dry land
And you long to be back on dry land

When those freezing night winds blow
And you're rocking to and fro
And it rains so hard that
You can't see your hands

You will feel you're all alone
Feel the fear knaw at your bones
Feel you heart a beatin' hard
To beat the band

Then you must know the river
Know how to give her
The respect she will more than demand
Know the river when your timbers shiver
And you long to be back on dry land
And you long to be back on dry land

EVERYTHING'S TRUE

All the letters they sent
Burning in the fire
True to their desires
Not a speck of regret
For the mischief of a liar
Foolishly admired

Rain on the window tastes like the sea
Birds in the birdbath bathing for tea
Love in her fingers reaching for you
Ashes to ashes everything's true

They gather today
In the hills outside of town
Where the poisons aren't allowed
They pattern their ways
By the movements of a cloud
Whose shadow stains the ground

Rain on the window tastes like the sea
Birds in the birdbath bathing for tea
Love in her fingers reaching for you
Ashes to ashes everything's true

Those who follow the trends
Say the signs are always there
Like a smile without a care
Of all the friends no longer there
I am nearer than the air

Rain on the window tastes like the sea
Birds in the birdbath bathing for tea
Love in her fingers reaching for you
Ashes to ashes everything's true

PAX

Pax is your name if you want it
It suits you like your blue baby bonnet
Our dream for you, you see
Is to live your life in peace
We love you, baby

There's nobody needing love
So much as those who
You'll want to shove
Remember it this way
Nobody is to blame
We love you, baby

Don't get stepped on
You aren't helping people
By being their slave
Stand up to them
With the power of love
Always

We are products of our being
Of everything we've seen
And what we're seeing
Every move's beyond control
Relax, it will unfold
We love you, baby

A Song For Everyone

Blue is the ocean yellow the sun
Wild is the river see how it runs
Bright is the moon that shines on the bay
Long are the hours short is the day

Where is the home I can call mine
Why should I search with nothing to find
Cold is the heart that hates what it loves
Hard is the hawk that sleeps with the dove

The movers and the shakers do it their way
Conquer the world with a gun
We'll get along singing a song for everyone

Gentle the sound that feels like a tear
Never too proud to be of good cheer
Slow is the dance that opens the heart
Stout is the lance that pierces the dark

THERE'S A HOLE IN MY LARIAT

I'm a lonesome cowboy
With horseshoes for my wheels
The nightwind for my blanket
It all seems so unreal
I beg you listen to me
Ride a mile in my chaps
And if the good Lord's willing
You won't fall into this trap

The dogies just get younger
While Old Paint is getting grey
He sighs beneath my weight
But he's too scared to say
What we've both been thinking
What we know is true
That I'm gonna have
To find somebody new

There's a hole in my lariat
Where the dogies ought to go
But how can I rope dogies
When the horse I ride's so slow
There's a hole in my lariat
As empty as the sky
You ain't seen nothin'
'til you seen a cowboy cry

They say poor workers
Try to blame their tools
But let me tell you partners
I'd get more done with a mule

All the girls are laughin'
Down at the saloon
Talkin' 'bout the fun they have
When they hear me croon

There's a hole in my lariat
Where the dogies ought to go
But how can I rope dogies
When the horse I ride's so slow
There's a hole in my lariat
As empty as the sky
You ain't seen nothin'
'til you seen a cowboy cry

A LONG LONG TIME AGO

Took a flight on the back of the night
A long long time ago
Took a stand on an ocean of sand
Why I did I'll never know

Ride on you broken angel
The sun is sinking low
How am I what I came to deny
A long long time ago
A long long time ago

Not surprised by the look in their eyes
A long long time ago
Life was cheap at the end of my feet
Where unknown shadows had to grow

Ride on you broken angel
The sun is sinking low
How am I what I came to deny
A long long time ago
A long long time ago

Such was I like a wheel on the fly
A long long time ago
Way behind with no shot at the line
Hobbled down a slippery road

Ride on you broken angel
The sun is sinking low
How am I what I came to deny
A long long time ago
A long long time ago

SWEET LITTLE SISTER

She's got a smile like
Our lovin' momma
Done tickled her eye
She's done nothin'
But laughin' since
She touched us with
Her sweet surprise

She's gone up so high
She's standing on the sky
She done fell in love
That sweet little sister of mine

Got the makins of a mother
Was the very line
They used to said
When she pushed me around
And said she's gonna bust my head

Now she's all grown up
She's sleepin' in
Another man's bed
She done fell in love
That sweet little sister of mine

I think it's fine she's
Found someone
To care for
If that ain't what
She's all about
I think I'm gonna lose my mind

151

She's got a smile like
Our lovin' momma
Done tickled her eye
She's done nothin'
But laughin' since
She touched us with
Her sweet surprise

She's gone up so high
She's standing on the sky
She done fell in love
That sweet little sister of mine

THE MOON IS GROWING OLD

Rise and shine in wounded time
The moon is growing old
Low down and swollen bound to burst
From what she holds so far above me
The moon is growing old

Rise and shine in wounded time
The moon is never new
I sing her song and her song
Is always blue so far above me
The moon is growing old

Alone in the night in wounded time
About to turn on a dime so far above me
The moon is growing old

Rise and shine in wounded time
All fragments of desire
Burn cross Heaven as sacraments
Of fire so far above me
The moon is growing old

Last time we met she had
A garden in her eyes
Filled with flowers you'd swear
Could never die so far above me
The moon is growing old

Alone in the night in wounded time
About to turn on a dime so far above me
The moon is growing old

Rise and shine in wounded time
The moon is never new
I sing her song and her song
Is always blue so far above me
The moon is growing old

THE BIBLE STRIKES AGAIN

They're killing people
In the land of the free
They're killing people 'cause
They got no right to be

They're killing people
In the land of the free
Lord have mercy,
Have mercy on me

An eye for an eye
And a prayer for a friend
That's what you get
When the Bible strikes again

An eye for an eye
And a prayer for a friend
That's what you get
When the Bible strikes again

They're killing people
In the land of the free
Lord have mercy,
Have mercy on me

MY MILK IS HOT AND READY

Just another coal train
Pumping black smoke down the line
Well, I better get a move on
But I have no sense of time

Everybody better call me
But please call me twice
Everybody better call me
And they better all be nice

My milk is hot and ready now
Body got a habit gonna keep until it goes
Well, if you want some answers
Better find somebody who knows

Just put away the wolf-trap
Tear the scaffold from your heart
Nobody in their right mind
Gonna try tell you apart

Sure pretty on the mountain
In the year above the pain
They say they got a fountain
Spits out manna tastes like rain

My milk is hot and ready now
Body got a habit gonna keep until it goes
Well, if you want some answers
Better find somebody who knows

My milk is hot, my milk is ready
My milk is hot, my milk is ready
My milk is hot, my milk is ready
My milk is hot, my milk is ready

WHAT A THRILL

What a thrill she is a mother
Caring for somebody other
Than this guy who is her lover
Now he's the daddy
Of their little laddie

What a thrill red as a berry
Doesn't have too many cares he
Only wants to have his momma
Hold him and feed him
And love him and need him

No one needs the daddy
He's helpless as a child
Nothing much to do but watch
Until after a while

What a thrill he is a poppa
Now it seems nothing can stop the
Flow of love coming to daddy
And momma from baby
So happy they're crazy

No one needs the daddy
He's helpless as a child
Nothing much to do but watch
Until after a while

What a thrill he is a poppa
Now it seems nothing can stop the
Flow of love coming to daddy
And momma from baby
So happy they're crazy

Nothin' Nobody Can Do

Passed a nomad down where no man
Talks about things he can do
I sat on the fence
They were changing the tense
Back to when it was shiny and new

I don't know but I been told
There's nothin' nobody can do
Nothin' nobody can do

Where's the fun in being young when
Everything withers in bloom
You grow up so fast
When you learn that what lasts
Is nowhere to be found in this room

I don't know but I been told
There's nothin' nobody can do
Nothin' nobody can do

All those lies under clear blue skies
When the world leaked out of you
Some sweet guise came and filled your eyes
With what you thought you had to do

Try to call it something solid
That which has no shadow don't move
Woven in stone
Cut so close to the bone
All that matters is shattered in two

I don't know but I been told
There's nothin' nobody can do
Nothin' nobody can do

WALKING ALL OVER THE WORLD

Fear and desire had gone away
Time meant nothing but a hill far away
Where snow was all that counted
And wounds were erased
And Old Man Winter had to cover his face

I spent what I had on what was there
The world kept turning and the road was bare
I climbed another mountain down to the sea
Where deep blue shadows had a hold on me

I followed my feet wherever they'd go
Dancing on top of the tips of my toes
I followed my feet wherever they'd go
Walking all over the world

I travelled far and I travelled wide
Ain't no different on the other side
Wherever I would wander, wherever I'd roam
Wherever I'm goin', I'm already home

I followed my feet wherever they'd go
Dancing on top of the tips of my toes
I followed my feet wherever they'd go
Walking all over the world

THE WAY OF THINGS

All along the morning they were dancing in the dark
Lost in restless fury with an action like a heart
Sad eyed and lonely they were waiting for a sign
To take their shadows to the broken edge of time

The living waters drowned the immigrants of fame
They made examples of those worthy of the name
Within the messages that screamed above the waves
Were well known passages forgotten from the page

That's the way of things
That's the song they sing
That's the way yay yay of things

Among the missing there were those they could not find
Bound down to nothing like a picture for the blind
Who knows what happened to the moments that they wore
Wild roses always grow behind an open door

That's the way of things
That's the song they sing
That's the way yay yay of things

They tried to listen to the wisdom of the night
But all the things they learned were moving out of sight
So glad you made it said the beggar to the king
You must be satisfied with losing everything

That's the way of things
That's the song they sing
That's the way yay yay of things

♪ THE KINDEST LIES

by Cynthia Atkins

John Lyle is a soulful and disciplined lyricist with an eye for the small details and nuances of daily life. His songs in *The Kindest Lies* catalog the joyful, heart-wrenching and self-deprecatingly human side of our natures.

The titles of each song offers a threshold into the interiors— We are led musically into reverie, cadence and rhymes that are surprising, inventive and lyrical. Lyle is a careful observer of human nature. These soulful narratives ring true with a range of dilemmas, that offer insight into our hearts and psyches.

Now I lay this ego down, put this mind to bed
Say good-bye to yesterday, while this sleepy head
Hears no one crying
Now I lay this ego down
While trumpet swans blow fanfares on the lake
For nobody's sake.

Lyle knows how to set the scene with color and dry wit. The lyrics engage all our senses with vivid pastoral tapestries. The words shed light on the rituals and desires that bring purpose and engagement to our lives. This language is vibrant and uniquely renders characters that live marginal and earthy lives, off the grid. Lyle songs are tender and passionate. The richness of his palette of sound is infectious. These sonorous vignettes are woven with details that permeate our ears and souls.

If I run out of atoms on the Santa-Fe
Think I'll pretend I'm Jimmy Rogers in a Chevrolet

Each song is inventive and compelling, not afraid to risk asking the big questions, or poke fun at the self. Lyles' voice is distinctive and metrical. The spare language makes us see the beauty of images, sounds and light—Each song shows us that *The Kindest Lies* are indelible and spirited. Lyle celebrates our quirky natures, our compassion and need for the palpable beauty, curiosity and magic of the world.

> *The snow lies heavy on the power line tonight*
> *I don't know where I'll find the strength to hold you tight.*

Cynthia Atkins
author of *Psyche's Weathers*
& *In the Event of Full Disclosure*

AFTERWORD

My love and thanks to Penny Lyle; a muse if ever there was one! And to Pax Lyle, Evelyn Thorogood, Jan Lyle and John Murray.

Without the efforts and encouragements of James Goddard, this book would certainly have not come to pass. Also, a special thanks to Seb Doubinsky who applied his own brand of encouragement to seal the deal.

Special thanks to Matt Bialer for his foreward to the book, and to Cynthia Atkins for her kind remarks about my work in her afterword 'The Kindest Lies.'

John Lyle

INDEX OF FIRST LINES

A

Above the rain like a child against a broken window pane	17
Against the drift of reason	28
All along the morning they were dancing in the dark	160
All locked into something the psychics can't control	97
All my roses refuse to tantalize	25
All the letters they sent	146

B

The biggest bully in the yard	49
Baby, rest beneath this tree	123
Blue is the ocean yellow the sun	147
By accident I took a double dose of L.S.D.	100

C

The carousel is finally winding down	45
The caveman was a rapist, no he wasn't very fair	122
Clean and pure as a mountain stream	59
Could be a story or it could be true	35
Cut-throat morons with their bloody horns and their bodies made of beer	22

D

The day of grace was up today, I'm shipwrecked in your arms	137
Darlin,' I been wonderin' about you	116
Dead man on a new horizon, colder than polarity	117
Do whales have scales? Do they go 'do-re-me' for so long,	48

E

Earth to Mother, here's a message from me	72
Every day of the week might as well be blue Monday	74
Evil forces gather in the half-light	50

F

Fear and desire had gone away   159

H

Higuey haircut's mighty fine   64

I

I am not an Indian from two hundred years ago   69
I asked her what she did for fun, she said she didn't know   57
I can see a day when this old earth will be a mess of tombs   119
I can't help it, I need another kiss   82
I can't read between the lines between the lines   135
If any one had said, hey, get to bed and beat your cold   114
If the sun don't burn the tears away from all our ragged dreams   133
If you're disappointed, the old man said to me   62
I know who I am, I know why I'm here   29
I'll bet nothing can get so small   60
I'm a lonesome cowboy   148
I may have been in China   52
I met her on the internet, we chatted through the night   75
I'm tired unto death from all these little knives   61
I must have missed it   37
I must say what must be said   79
In and out and out and in   98
Inga said a mouthful when she said   51
In the city of love, the cops don't use a gun   41
In the shadow of the wasteland in the desert of the heart   21
In the wreckage of our love the black box can't be found   73
I should be committed   80
I thought I saw you where the weeping willows grow   18
It's clear to me that countries are in business to survive   115
I wish that I was one of Katherine Ross's hosses   129

J

Job had some issues he couldn't comprehend   70
Just another coal train   156

L

Let's stop our foolin' around   111
Life is a breeze when we're down by the sea   108
Like a faded leaf, hanging by a thread   53
Love is hot, love is cold   24
Love lies bleeding, in the death of night   39

M

The mind is deep and quiet   94
Missed a lot of lovin' down in Tennessee   128
My ancestors were amphibian   107
My guts are tied in knots my eyes are filled with clay   40
My heart's been sent to heaven   131

N

Neon Bride, please come inside, you've sanctified the street   127
No one knows where minutes go to while away the hours   23
Now I lay me down, with a sigh   76

O

Oh the wind is like a friend of mine, she is fickle to a fault   99
Old Joe calls from the hill   58
On the trail of broken hearts   85
Outside The Golden Lantern hoboes wear no clothes   19

P

Passed a nomad down where no man   158
Pax is your name if you want it   146

R

Reverberating into the innermost reaches of his private brain   130
Rise and shine in wounded time   153

S

7:30 and another dirty show to go and see   110
A sentimental wishing well where the bubbles never stop   92
Scientologists are coming, there's a Mormon at the door   46
She's got a smile like   151
She wore the scarlet letter like a chain   20
So many times, you've buttressed the mind   83
Someone said that you have gone bone dry   34
Someone's calling through the wind and the rain   91

T

There's a mine in the hill   71
They're killing people   155
Things are getting' boring 'cause my wife just caught me snoring   120
This little bubble, this black cauldron of trouble   103
Those who will be free put their faith in me   81
Took a flight on the back of the night   150

W

Was a mourning dove in the old grey window   26
Way past now, past the burning cow   65
We have ranchero, we have mucho dinero   104
Well, I know your lazy susans, and I know your easy chairs   132
We must know what really happened (gonna tell ya)   101
What a thrill she is a mother   157
What a thrill to climb over the hill   113
When I'm a P.H.D., no one will dare to question me   102
When our trust is in the gambler and the odds are on the wall   134
When the apple is ripe it will fall   93
Where you goin', darlin' daughter, didn't your Daddy raise
you right?   87

Y

You Broke Right Down and Cried   141
You felt you had to post   143
You're a funny funny animal,   38
You're the captain of your craft   144
You scream around the corner, like Little Jack Horner   47
You were nameless   141
You were sitting by a river   33

Index Of Song Titles

A Break in the Weather   143
A Breath of Light   39
A Dog Lies Down Sometime   47
A Little Bit of Heaven On a Saturday Night   70
A Long Long Time Ago   150
A New Bandana   22
A Song For Everyone   147
Above the Rain   17
All That Binds   94
Another Golden Dream   25
Being the Things You Do   83
Blasted in Hope   98
Blind Love   50
Blood River   107
Blue Pictures in the Tunnel   110
Bone Dry   34
Bound and Determined   37
Centers   60
City of Love   41
Close Your Eyes   123
Country Harvest Time   93
Deathless Song   133
Do Whales Have Scales   48
Don't String Up the Throwback   122
Earth to Mother   72
Everything's True   145
Funny, Funny Animal   38
Going Through the Motions   103
Gunfight at the Occult Corral   117
Hello Buddy   132
Higuey Haircut   64
Hold On As She Goes   19

Hope Signals	69
How Romantic of Me	97
I Know Who I Am	29
I Know You Rider	35
I Lost My Sense Of Humour	79
I Need Another Kiss	82
I Saw God	100
I Should Be Commited	80
I Thought I Saw You	18
I Won't Be Lonesome When I'm Gone	52
In the Wreckage of Our Love	73
Just My Kind of Girl	57
Katherine Ross's Hosses	129
Keep the Banners Flying	131
Know the River	144
Lies Are Only Letters	130
Life is a Breeze	108
Like a Blank	40
Little Knives	61
Living Through the Blues	128
Lonesome Daddy Blues	74
Lose	135
Lost in the Dream	137
Love Is	24
My Addled Essence	111
My Cold is Gone	114
My Love is Everything	59
My Milk is Hot and Ready	156
Native Son of the First Cause	115
No One Knows	23
Nothin' Nobody Can Do	158
Now I Lay Me Down	76
Oh, My Wind	99
Old Hontana Road	51
Old Joe Calls From the Hill	58
On the Trail Of Broken Hearts	85
Open Wide	28
Pax	146
Pay Me No Mind	75
Ranchero	104
Rivers of Stone	127
Shadow of the Wasteland	21
Someone's Calling	91

Sparkling River   53
Straight On Down the Line   92
Sweet Little Sister   151
The Bible Strikes Again   155
The Camel's Back   62
The Guru's Lament   81
The Kindest Lies   161
The Moon is Growing Old   153
The Mourning Dove   26
The Plot Widens   119
The Showdown Might Be Tragedy   134
The Walls of Jericho   27
The Way of Things   160
The Woo Woo Into Town   120
There's a Hole in My Lariat   148
They Stoned Her   20
Too Much Compassion   49
Turn Your Lamp Down, Momma   71
Walk It On Down   46
Walking All Over the World   159
Water Works   113
Way Past Now   65
We All Fall Down   33
We Must Know   101
What a Thrill   157
When I'm a P. H. D.   102
When the Wind Gets High   45
Where You Goin', Darlin' Daughter   87
Wonderin'   116
You Broke Right Down and Cried   141

www.ingramcontent.com/pod-product-compliance
Lightning Source LLC
LaVergne TN
LVHW011420080426
835512LV00005B/165